DO NOTHING!

'Combining real-world examples with cutting-edge research, *Do Nothing!* provides counterintuitive insights and connects them to practical solutions. After reading this book, you will do less but achieve more'
Adam Galinsky, Morris and Alice Kaplan Professor of Ethics and Decision in Management

'No leader will read this book without seriously considering his or her leadership style. The advice and insights are based on solid research, and the ideas are novel, fascinating'
Max H. Bazerman, Jesse Isidor Straus Professor of Business Administration, Harvard Business School; co-author of *Blind Spots* and *Negotiation Genius*

'Murnighan has identified that contrary to popular opinion, leadership turns out to be as much about what you don't do as what you do'
Glen Tullman, CEO, Allscripts

'Murnighan has delivered an interesting, new, and sometimes counterintuitive way to look at what can make a great leader'
John Rex-Waller, CEO, National Surgical Hospitals

'*Do Nothing!* provides a unique and counterintuitive approach to running a business . . . This valuable guide will help everyone who reads it to manage better and accomplish more'
Michael Reinsdorf, president, Chicago Bulls

ABOUT THE AUTHOR

J. Keith Murnighan is an award-winning professor at the Kellogg School of Management, and teaches organizational behaviour, psychology and economics in the US, UK and around the world. He has advised major organizations such as Pfizer and DHL, Ernst & Young and Motorola, and his research is regularly cited by the international media, including the *Economist* and the *Wall Street Journal*.

*How to Stop
Overmanaging
and Become a
Great Leader*

DO
NOTHING!

J. Keith Murnighan

PORTFOLIO
PENGUIN

PORTFOLIO PENGUIN

Published by the Penguin Group
Penguin Books Ltd, 80 Strand, London WC2R 0RL, England
Penguin Group (USA) Inc., 375 Hudson Street, New York, New York 10014, USA
Penguin Group (Canada), 90 Eglinton Avenue East, Suite 700, Toronto, Ontario,
Canada M4P 2Y3 (a division of Pearson Penguin Canada Inc.)
Penguin Ireland, 25 St Stephen's Green, Dublin 2, Ireland
(a division of Penguin Books Ltd)
Penguin Group (Australia), 707 Collins Street,
Melbourne, Victoria 3008, Australia (a division of Pearson Australia Group Pty Ltd)
Penguin Books India Pvt Ltd, 11 Community Centre,
Panchsheel Park, New Delhi – 110 017, India
Penguin Group (NZ), 67 Apollo Drive, Rosedale, Auckland 0632, New Zealand
(a division of Pearson New Zealand Ltd)
Penguin Books (South Africa) (Pty) Ltd, Block D, Rosebank Office Park,
181 Jan Smuts Avenue, Parktown North, Gauteng 2193, South Africa

Penguin Books Ltd, Registered Offices: 80 Strand, London WC2R 0RL, England

www.penguin.com

First published in the United States of America by Portfolio/Penguin,
a member of Penguin Group (USA) Inc. 2012
First published in Great Britain by Portfolio Penguin 2012
This edition published 2013
002

Printed in Great Britain by Clays Ltd, St Ives plc

A CIP catalogue record for this book is available from the British Library

ISBN: 978-0-670-92199-7

www.greenpenguin.co.uk

Penguin Books is committed to a sustainable
future for our business, our readers and our planet.
This book is made from Forest Stewardship
Council™ certified paper.

This book is dedicated to

Mom, Dad, and Beth

Kev, Tom, and Peg

the kinds of leaders we should all emulate

Contents

Preface   ix

1 Do Nothing!   1

2 Focus on Them   21

3 Start at the End   55

4 Trust More   77

5 Release Control (Deviously)   105

6 Bear Down Warmly   125

7 Ignore Performance Goals   137

8 De-emphasize Profits   157

9 Unnatural Leaders   171

Acknowledgments   201

Bibliography   205

Index   215

Preface

THIS BOOK IS all about your natural tendencies and when they can lead you astray. Most of our natural tendencies are pretty wonderful: they have repeatedly helped us get out of tight spots and, bottom line, they have allowed us to survive and even thrive.

The problem is that some of our natural tendencies are no longer effective. Our ancestors were hunters and gatherers whose existence depended on their natural drive for self-preservation: they developed tendencies and strategies that were evolutionarily effective and they passed them down from generation to generation until they eventually landed in us. In the last thousand years, however, civilization and technology have advanced far faster than we have evolved, making some of our natural tendencies obsolete. Developing the ability to formulate strategies that consistently resulted in finding sources of food and nourishment, for instance, was an incredibly smart approach to life thousands of years ago, but these kinds of skills are much less relevant in today's increasingly urban world.

We can't escape our ancestors, however, and the influence that their successes have had on the way we live our lives. In particular, they endowed us with a natural inclination to actively pursue our goals—so much so that not acting feels terribly wrong. This legacy is tremendously helpful—until we become leaders. Then our natural tendencies to act lead us to do too much. This is the curse of overmanaging, and far too many leaders fall under its spell. *Do Nothing!* shows you why you must fight this natural tendency, both in your thoughts and in your actions. It also includes summaries of a host of findings from research in the social sciences that documents its negative effects.

This book is for you and everyone else you know who is called on to lead. Leaders have a tremendous, trickle-down impact on scores of people: one great leader can have a host of positive effects on hundreds, sometimes thousands of people. Organizations are reflections of their leaders, and if their leaders can be more effective and avoid overmanaging, many, many people will benefit.

Do Nothing! focuses on leaders at the top, the middle, and the bottom of organizations—in other words, leaders of all kinds, with a specific focus on leaders and their immediate teams. I am particularly interested in the leaders of relatively small groups of people who interact on a regular basis. *Do Nothing!* does not try to present ideas that will allow CEOs to have a direct impact on every one of the 83,000 employees in their organizations. Instead, it focuses more on the thoughts and actions of leaders and their team members, CEOs and their top management teams, executives and their closest contacts, middle managers and the groups that look to them for leadership, and you and the people you work with most. If more and more leaders of more and more teams start doing less and, as a result, start being more and more effective, the overall impact could be incredible.

Do Nothing! includes a series of interconnected, counterintuitive ideas that can help you think differently, act differently, and lead differently, in ways that are not particularly natural. If there are just a few golden nuggets here—ideas that you can really use to be more effective—that will be great. And maybe, just maybe, you will return to this book next year, five years from now, or even twenty-five years from now, and pick up another useful idea or two that will help you simultaneously do less and be more effective.

In the end, *Do Nothing!* is about making other people's lives better and, as a nice by-product, yours, too. By all means let me know if you find it useful, as well as how you've used it to be more effective. Thanks.

J. Keith Murnighan
EVANSTON, ILLINOIS
AUGUST 2011

DO NOTHING!

Do Nothing!

*L*ET'S START WITH a dream. You have just come back
to work after a three-week vacation. You had time to
see some of the members of your extended family and
some old friends; you spent a week relaxing at the beach; and you
also mixed in a couple side trips to see old ruins and amazing
terrain. You didn't take your cell phone and you didn't check
e-mail the whole time you were gone. You returned home last
night, and this morning you have come to work a bit early, thinking that there might be a lot to do. As you were sorting through
your mail, the members of your team arrived, at their normal
times. They walked by your desk, waved, said "hello" and "welcome back," and asked whether you had a good time. Then they
trundled off to do their jobs.

Throughout the morning, you discovered that there are no
pressing issues. Not only that—during your absence, the team
scored a big new customer and fixed a nagging problem. Some
of your peers in other teams commented that your team members seem very committed, and they seem to be particularly

focused today as well, even when they are working by themselves. In fact, when you check on the status of your team's various projects, you find that you are ahead of schedule on all but a few. In other words, work is proceeding extremely well.

Sounds wonderful, doesn't it? Sadly, for most leaders it is only a dream—a nice dream, but only a dream. The reality for most people is that they never take a vacation for as long as three continuous weeks and, if they did, they would take their cell phone, and their laptop, so that they could constantly check on what's happening back at the office, even when they didn't really need to; and when they returned to work they would expect the worst, fearing that, because of their absence, the team and their tasks had devolved into chaos and they should never have left in the first place, not even for a day. In other words, for most leaders, their version of reality is more like a nightmare than a dream.

The everyday life of a leader is rarely calm. Their workdays tend to be hectic, fragmented, and fast-paced: finishing everything never happens. Leaders come to work early and leave late; they bring work home with them; they work on weekends—they feel like they have to, just to keep up. This creates enormous pressure, as they see themselves as the most critical members of their teams, the ones who are most responsible for every team member's outcomes. Many of their team members don't help, either, as they often look to their leaders to provide critical solutions.

How do leaders respond to this enormous pressure? Their natural reaction is to do more—to do everything that they possibly can. They complain that there are not enough hours in the day ("if only I had more time"), as if they didn't work extremely hard already.

These observations lead to a simple conclusion: conscientious, dedicated leaders do too much—way too much.

All of us have encountered workaholics—people who define

themselves by their success, who don't feel fulfilled unless they are putting in exceedingly long hours, and who don't seem to know that life might actually exist outside of their work.

But we are not talking about workaholics here; we are talking about your normal, everyday, hardworking, achievement-oriented leader. The critical issue here goes beyond workaholics—this is about leaders who love and value their families more than their jobs; who delight in hanging out with their friends and not doing much of anything when they can; who are happy to relax and chill out. This is about people who are accomplished and smart and who work hard, but not to the exclusion of all else. These kinds of people *still* get sucked into what they think are the demands of being a great leader, of feeling like they need to be reachable 24/7, of believing that they are responsible for every single thing their team members do.

As you have probably guessed, this book takes a very different approach to leadership. Most leaders clearly try to do way too much at work; not only that, because they try to do too much, they perform worse than they otherwise could—and their teams don't perform as well as they could either.

There is a solution, however. It is far simpler than you might have imagined. Two words:

DO NOTHING!

Yes, nothing. Crazy? Suicidal? Extreme? Maybe. But consider what would happen if you actually took this simple advice and did nothing. You would come to work each day, say hello to the members of your team, see how they are doing, and then you would do very little else. If you actually did this, what would happen?

In physics, a vacuum is particularly fragile: to survive, it must be contained. If it is not contained, other elements will be drawn to it and will fill the space that it previously filled.

Effective teams work the same way: when chances to excel appear, people want to fill them. Consider an old story about Eastman Kodak Company. After a massive reorganization, a small division was inadvertently left without a leader and without any reporting lines to headquarters. No one in the division seemed to mind. They just continued to do their work, effectively and efficiently, *for months*. In fact, the top executives at Kodak forgot that they even existed. It took a note to headquarters from a happy customer, thanking the group for their excellent work, before the head honchos realized that this entire division had been "lost" and left on its own. The beauty of this situation, of course, is that the people in this division knew their jobs and did them—they filled the vacuum, and they acted as if they had never needed a leader. They did just fine on their own.

"That wouldn't happen with my team" might be your immediate, natural reply. But if this is what you were thinking, there is an obvious follow-up question:

How do you know?

The answer, of course, is also obvious: you can't know since you haven't tried it.

The point here is simple: why not try it? *Do Nothing—and see if the vacuum gets filled.* My experience suggests that you will be surprised—wildly surprised. People on your team will reveal skills you never knew they had, and will accomplish things that go far beyond your estimate of their capabilities. They might not do things the way you would do them, but they will get results you never expected—positive results—because everyone has hidden talents, and most leaders never discover them.

Before you reject this approach immediately, ask yourself again: what if you did nothing and it actually worked?

The Key

The key insight here is simple: you will be a more effective leader if, rather than doing the work yourself, you let other people do it. In other words, stop working and start leading.

Some basic examples: engineers who take over an engineering team stop doing basic design; RNs who run employment agencies that provide part-time nurses to hospitals no longer work directly with patients; and CEOs of Fortune 500 companies rarely do their own taxes or mow their own lawns. Nor should they. As you move up in the world, people will look to you to think big thoughts and orchestrate the big issues; they will want you to use broad brushstrokes rather than focusing on details—even if you are really good at being a detail person.

Unfortunately, we naturally anchor on what we have been doing in our current jobs, and we tend to take great comfort in the status quo. Although we may have strong desires to move up in the world, fear, uncertainty, and at least a little anxiety accompany the idea of every upward job change. The "status quo bias" is a pervasive tendency for people to like their current state and to be resistant to change. This even affects people who have just been promoted— they may love the fact that they have been promoted but they still find themselves reminiscing, at least some of the time, about how great it was "in the good old days, when things were simpler." Things *are* simpler when other people are in charge and you don't have to make big decisions. Taking over as a leader means that you must depart from the comfort of the status quo, and the anxiety, fear, and uncertainty that accompany your excitement really are noxious. To avoid these feelings, people naturally fall back on what's familiar and certain—that is, what they know how to do. Unfortunately, this can be truly counterproductive.

Think, for instance, of technicians who get promoted to manage other technicians. This may be a welcome promotion, a big step on the road to managerial success. One of the biggest problems for these new manager-leaders is their natural urge to exercise their technical skills. Their promotion represents a *fundamental* change, however, from the world of technology to the world of leadership. Its simplest manifestation is that they must now let other people do the technical stuff: they need to be leaders and use their technical expertise less.

People who ignore this maxim seem to suffer from an old concept called the Peter Principle: they advance to a level and then appear to be incompetent. It's not that they don't have the skills to succeed in their new position—it's that they feel so comfortable using their old, established skills that they often have a hard time changing. Once you've been promoted, you must play a whole new ball game. Successful leaders must shift gears and, literally, do less of what they used to do, even though they were good at it.

A simple solution to this problem can allow you to succeed at doing less: figure out who among your team members is good at a particular job *and let them do it*—even if it's something that you can do well.

I was never the greatest of students. But some of the things I learned in school have stuck with me for a long time. In high school, in a single term on economics, I learned about the potent concept of *comparative advantage*. Here's how it works: when a team is faced with a task, they must determine who does what so that they can complete the task effectively and efficiently. Complex tasks may require the team members to complete a number of interrelated subtasks. If there is a key subtask that only one person is good at, she should be the person who is assigned to that task—even if she is also the best person at another subtask. The logic of comparative advantage rests on the fact that poor performance on a critical subtask can sink the entire project and, if two people can perform a particular task, you may not need the very best performer for it, especially if they are needed somewhere else and the alternate is good enough. (This fits a wise and important saying: "Don't let perfect interfere with good enough.")

The moral of this story is particularly important for leaders: your comparative advantage, as a leader, is *not* to get involved in doing different jobs. Instead, you must focus on facilitating others' performance and orchestrating their actions so that they combine their efforts into the most effective final product. If you can let your team members work on jobs that they can do, they will feel better about what they are doing, they will grow and do more, and you will be able to do other things.

Here's some additional intuition: team members whose leaders do too much see them as micromanagers—but micromanagers never think that they micromanage. As a result, they continue to micromanage, alienating their team members even more and doing far worse as a team than they otherwise could.

This problem is easy to avoid: let people do their work. Have your best writer write the first draft of an important report; have your most persuasive team member make your team's next pitch; and have your most anal, detail-oriented person check out every detail before you go public. *Don't do any of these things yourself.* Instead, help people succeed in what they are doing. Spend your time and efforts facilitating *their* performance: provide your writer with the best information available so she can put it all together in a neat, coherent package; give your best salespeople as many insights about your potential new customer as you and your team can provide so that they can mold their pitch to satisfy the new customer's most important needs; and let your pickiest nitpicker have at your team's most recent efforts to ensure that no one is wearing blinders that will embarrass everyone if someone else points out your team's fatal flaws before you do.

This is what great leaders do. They don't work; they facilitate and orchestrate. They think of great strategies and help other people implement them. They spend their time on achieving the foresight to be able to see new developments as or just before they happen. They take a broad, comprehensive view of their terrain while they also notice some of the key details so they can confidently choose the best of many possible forks in the road. They don't do anything—except think, make key decisions, help people do their jobs better, and add a touch of organizational control to make sure the final recipes come out okay.

Leaders who are too busy working, doing a job, can't do these things—and their teams suffer.

Doing too much is far worse than doing too little. When leaders do too much, they cannot be as effective or as thoughtful or as strategic as they might otherwise be. Even worse, their team members are underutilized and underchallenged. Better team members are also likely to be increasingly angry—because their leader is doing what they could and should and want to be doing. By not letting good performers do their jobs, *on their own*, leaders don't allow their team members to feel proud of what they can do. The end result is the development of dislike or even hate for a leader who butts in, as well as earning him a reputation for being a control freak and a micromanager.

Doing Nothing is not easy for people who like their work and are driven to succeed. It is also not easy for people whose ancestors had to work hard just to survive. But if you can get yourself to *Do Nothing*, you will soon find that your team members will grow as a team, and you will grow as a leader. *You just have to get out of their way.* This is not a natural approach to work, especially for people who have achieved their leadership positions because they were outstanding performers in their previous jobs.

At this point you may still be saying to yourself, "I must do something. I didn't get to this exalted leadership position by doing nothing. Surely there is something that I could and should do, isn't there?" This is a perfectly natural question.

Here's what you can actually do: to be a truly effective leader, you should be a *facilitator* and an *orchestrator*. Rather than doing work that your team members can do, help them do their jobs better. Facilitate their performance rather than interfering with it. Then add a touch of orchestration, to make sure that Annie finishes her work before William does his so that everything will be ready at the right time. When you facilitate and orchestrate well, your team members will work well, individually and collectively.

When things are really clicking, work will be like the performance of a great Beethoven symphony, with the notes in the right place, the crescendos coming on time, and at the end, a feeling of exhilaration at your collective accomplishments. Leaders and their teams *never* experience this kind of thrill when leaders do too much.

Here's some more intuition: How would it feel if all of your team members were living up to their maximum potential? What would your life be like?

I've asked hundreds (if not thousands) of leaders these two questions. Their universal, almost identical response starts non-verbally, with a big smile that emerges slowly. Life as a leader becomes pretty wonderful when your team members are all performing as well as they possibly can.

This insight should help leaders think of their jobs differently. A leader's job is *not* to do things. Instead, leaders do best when they help other people do as much as they can as well as they can. If each and every member of a team lives up to their maximum potential, the team and its leader will be as successful as they can possibly be.

If you follow this advice, it will make your life easier, and just think what it will do for your team members: they will perform better, they will feel better about themselves, the team will be more effective, and everyone will benefit—even people who are less excited about their jobs. (Everyone has a spark of pride somewhere, particularly because we invest so much time working. For some people this spark is hard to find. But many people take great pride in doing their jobs well. More on this later.)

It's Not Easy

Doing Nothing sounds easy, but for too many people, it isn't, and being a facilitator doesn't always come naturally either. Most leaders move up through the ranks by displaying their skills and by doing a great job at what they do. Performance—doing things—distinguishes those who move up from those who don't. The difficult part for many leaders—and what too many leaders don't see—is that, as you move up, *your* performance becomes less important than *your team's performance*, and for your team to do better, you must do less, in ever-increasing fashion, with every promotion. The logical end point of continuously doing less is to do nothing at all.

This doesn't happen enough. It's not easy for type-A leaders to *Do Nothing*. Take, for example, the story of a student in one of my executive MBA classes. Dan called me one day and said, "Keith, I have great news. I just got promoted to run our IT department." I congratulated him and told him I was proud of him as this was a big, early promotion. Then he said, in a lower, quieter tone, "I have one problem. I really love doing IT and now that I am running the department, I'm not sure that I'll be able to use my skills anymore."

My response was immediate: I told Dan that his promotion was tremendous, that he had been hoping for something like this for some time, that he should be ecstatic, and that he was right, he wasn't going to be able to do IT anymore.

For the next thirty-five minutes, the two of us repeated the same two ideas: he kept saying how much he loved doing IT, and I kept saying that this was too bad and that he couldn't do it anymore. Occasionally we changed the wording, but we kept repeating this same story, over and over. He really didn't want to give up the skills he had worked so hard to perfect.

His predicament is true of every leader: when you get promoted, you can't rely on your technical skills anymore. Your world has changed; you are no longer a technician; you have to manage and, better yet, you have to lead.

Dan succeeded in not doing IT, but he didn't succeed right away. He had the good fortune of running a department of truly talented people. For the first few months, he stuck his toes into various projects and did a little IT work—he just couldn't resist. All too often, he would be reviewing the progress of his programmers and he would jump on their keyboards and add a bit here or a bit there, thinking that he was helping them refine their work. This was particularly frustrating for Dan's best people: they did their jobs well and, even though their approach was a little different from Dan's, their results were just as good. They not only felt that Dan was meddling in their jobs, they complained among themselves that he was micromanaging.

Whenever Dan butted in, he always smiled and said, "Let me show you what I mean." Ultimately this led to one of his best people leaving the company to take another job, "because there I can do my own thing." Dan tried hard to keep him, but it was too late. Losing this person's skills was a serious blow to the team, but Dan more than made up for it with a tremendous gain—he finally realized that he had to stop meddling in his team members' jobs. He had to stop doing IT—cold turkey—even though he loved it.

Luckily, his story has a positive ending, and Dan has lived happily ever since. His problem, though, is all too common: he had skills that he couldn't help wanting to use. He was rewarded for using them, too, as his team members and his superiors often complimented him on the job that he was doing in IT, *before* his promotion to manager. Once he took a leadership role, however, he was *never* praised for his IT skills, by anyone. Instead he needed to put those wonderfully useful skills on a shelf and shift gears—radically. It wasn't easy, but not making this change would have put tremendous limits on his future advancement.

Most people don't make this shift easily. As in Dan's case, there are almost always bumps in the road, sometimes big bumps, before they get the picture. And some people never do.

Potential Downsides

There are times when even the best leaders cannot and should not *Do Nothing*. Two are particularly common.

Number 1: When you are the only one with the skills needed for an urgent task. With time pressure and no one else capable of performing a necessary task, it is obvious that leaders must roll up their sleeves and step in.

But ideally, this should happen only once. Anytime your team members don't have all of the skills that are needed to complete a job, you must see if you can arrange training for them so they can take over the next time this kind of task surfaces.

This will help them expand their skill sets and allow them to feel that their responsibilities have expanded. At the same time, you can move back to Doing Nothing and leading your team.

If no one on your team has the ability to gain the necessary skills, it pays to consider whether it is worthwhile for your organization to hire someone who does. In tight economies and small companies, even the big bosses must sometimes roll up their sleeves and do a job. But these are not ideal situations and, for successful companies, they should be temporary.

Number 2: When dirty work needs to be done, everyone should take their turn, including leaders. I define "dirty work" as any job that no one wants to do. (Thus, in a literal sense, it doesn't have to involve dirt.) Every team has dirty work. The ideal approach to dirty work is to set up a rotation with you, the leader of the team, taking your turn just like everyone else. Loading all the dirty work onto one or two people makes their jobs too heavy; it can also create immediate and long-standing resentment. Also, not including yourself in the rotation can encourage your team members to think that you have put yourself on a pedestal above them—not a good thing.

The ideal solution in a dirty work rotation scheme is for your team members to push you out of the rotation and demand that they take your place. This choice, however, is completely up to them, and even the best teams might hate dirty work so much that they let you take your turn.

These may be the only times that require a team leader to actually get into work and do a job. Even these two instances, however, can ultimately resolve themselves so that leaders can ultimately *Do Nothing*.

The idea that a leader can play golf every day and not show up for work is obviously fallacious. Effective leaders facilitate and orchestrate: they keep track of what their team is doing to make sure that the job gets done, but they don't impose and they obviously don't micromanage (or even come close). Instead, they structure situations that allow people to excel and to be committed to their teams, their jobs, and their organizations.

Another downside people often worry about when they contemplate doing nothing is the fear of being seen as lazy. Leaders who actually *Do Nothing* realize that this is not a realistic fear. But fears are not rational, and leaders who are trying to cut back on their activities often think that other people will see them doing nothing and think that they are *literally* doing nothing.

The beauty of the philosophy behind Doing Nothing is that you only get to *Do Nothing* when your team members are performing well, and when your team members are performing well, they will be doing their jobs—and who will get the credit for it? If you're not careful, you will. In fact, even if you are careful, you will. Teams are *always* reflections of their leaders, and their successes always create a positive glow for the team's leaders, even if they seemed to *Do Nothing* to achieve it.

Thus, if your team is successful and people see that you are Doing Nothing, they will not think of you as lazy. Instead, they will want to know your secret. "How does she do it?" will be a common refrain, because too many people don't realize that they could be far more successful by Doing Nothing, too.

What Will You Do While You Are Doing Nothing?

If you succeed in Doing Nothing, how will you spend your time at work? First of all, you will have time to plan for the future—an unusual luxury. Next, as we've noted, you can work to facilitate your team members' performance, and you can do that without really doing anything yourself. As you facilitate, you should have high expectations for their performance: by expecting a lot from your people, you will generally get a lot. This is what researchers have called the Pygmalion effect.

Pygmalion was a fictional character in the *Metamorphoses*, Ovid's narrative poem about the history of the world up until Julius Caesar's time; he finished writing it in A.D. 8. Pygmalion was a sculptor who was not attracted to the local women, as many of them were prostitutes. Instead, he fell in love with a statue he had made of a woman. At Venus's festival, he made offerings to the goddess and asked (hopefully) for his statue to be turned into a real woman. Venus sent Cupid to kiss the sculpture's hand, transforming it into a beautiful woman whom Pygmalion ultimately married. In other words, he was one lucky guy.

Pygmalion also had really high expectations. As a result, his name is now associated with an effect researchers have frequently observed: the high expectations of an authority figure—traditionally, the instructor in a classroom—can lead individuals to perform better than they would have if the leader/teacher did not expect so much from them. In essence, when a leader expects a lot, team members typically respond in kind. Why? In large part because high expectations, even when they are not warranted, change how the teachers themselves behave.

Teachers do all sorts of positive things for their high-expectation students: they pay more attention to them; they praise them and encourage them more; they reward and punish them more; they call on them more in class discussions; they talk with them more; and they are more accepting, positive, and supportive of them. They are also biased in how they evaluate them.

It makes sense for leaders to emulate these effective teachers.

In studies on adults, Pygmalion effects have been strongest for people in the military, among men, and in situations where leaders start with initially low expectations.

Several Pygmalion studies have been conducted in the Israeli Defense Forces. In one, soldiers were enrolled in a fifteen-week course on combat command. Their instructors were told that all of the soldiers had taken a highly reliable set of tests and had received ratings by previous instructors on their command potential. The results of the tests indicated that one third of the group of soldiers—randomly chosen, so they were actually no better or worse than anyone else in the course—had scored "High" and were expected to excel in the course, as well as in their careers as commanders. Another third had supposedly achieved a score of "Regular" and were expected to do well but not extremely well. A final third were not classified due to "a shortage of data."

Fifteen weeks later, at the end of the course, the High-score soldiers took a battery of tests and achieved scores that were 22.7 percent better than those of the Regulars. Their attitudes toward the course were also 46.3 percent more positive than the Regulars'; they even felt that their instructors had displayed more leadership, by 22.9 percent.

Effective leaders can get the same kinds of effects. In particular, teams can benefit enormously when their leaders have high, positive expectations. This should be a consistent message. It's also a message that you don't have to convey verbally. If you consistently have high standards and you are committed to them, your team members will get the message and will do their best to reach them. And getting this message across doesn't require that you do anything—your team members will get a good sense of how you feel from your everyday, high-standard activities.

The Bottom Line

When you get promoted to a leadership position, you must give up your past—a past that you have worked extremely hard to create—and do less and less so that you can achieve more. Too many leaders do way too much. When they do too much, they are not doing their new job—instead, they are doing *their old job,* and

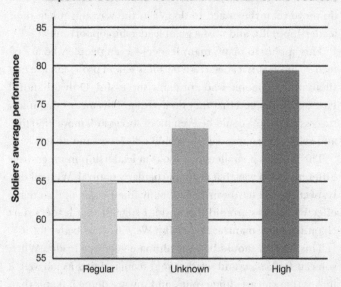

Expected Command Potential at the Start of the Course

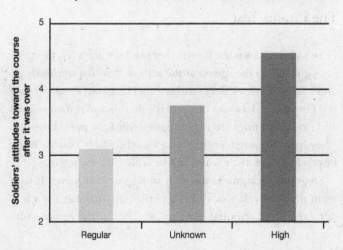

Expected Command Potential at the Start of the Course

they block their team members' chances to flourish. Leaders who do more than they need to do get in the way, misutilize their leadership skills, and miss a great leadership opportunity.

This applies to many, many leaders—even people who are effective, successful leaders. As a business school professor, I've met thousands of people who are really successful. Only a handful have acknowledged that they do nothing. This means that many successful people could be even more successful, more effective, and achieve even more if they could only let go and do less.

This book is a challenge: it looks at leadership in an entirely different way, a way that is not particularly natural. With all due respect for the hard work of so many fine people and so many effective leaders around the world, I suggest that leaders start chanting a new mantra: *Do Nothing!* We will all be better for it.

This mantra should be your ultimate goal as a leader. When you can *Do Nothing* and see that your team is doing its job well, it means that you are doing yours, and you are doing it better than when you did too much.

The Litmus Test

Here's a final litmus test for whether you have achieved this goal. Let's go back to the dream at the start of this chapter. You were on vacation for three weeks without checking your e-mail or your cell phone. Leaders who can actually do this and return to work and find that things are running smoothly have passed the test. They have become truly effective leaders. There's also a lovely by-product here: their teams will be truly effective teams.

So go on vacation. Leave your work phone at home. If your team needs to call you, this is a perfect opportunity for a test: don't reply and see what they can do. They might surprise you, and they might even surprise themselves. Not only that, they might never call at all.

Does this strike fear into your heart? Or does it just seem impossible? It doesn't have to be. Set your sights on Doing Nothing, and you may find yourself being able to take a truly wonderful and completely relaxing vacation. How does that sound?

Focus on Them

*I*NFORMATION IS POWER. This is a truism that is not universally true: research indicates that, when people know that they have disproportionately more power than other people do, they don't always use it. (Think, for example, of benevolent dictators.) But having information can be really useful, for leaders and people in general. The process of getting information, however, is sometimes a challenge, especially when you're trying to get information from an adversary.

Getting information from an opponent or an enemy is not as simple as just asking a direct question and getting an accurate answer. People involved in combat have long faced this problem: when they capture an opponent, they hope to persuade him to reveal information that will further their cause and increase the probability of capturing his comrades (their enemies). As a result, combat soldiers have become extremely creative in their information acquisition techniques, sometimes using the "third degree." Physical beatings, however, result in bruises and other visible evidence that can get questioners into trouble. Thus, to avoid recriminations, many interrogators have used less obvious techniques; for a long time, one of their favorite tools has been water.

In fact, various forms of waterboarding have been around since the trials of the Spanish Inquisition in the 1500s. Its basic methodology involves having a person lie down with their feet slightly higher than their head, covering their face with a cloth, and pouring water over the cloth to induce a feeling of drowning.

Is this technique torture or is it an acceptable interrogation technique? In 2002 and 2003, the director of the CIA admitted that the agency had used waterboarding on three suspected terrorists and a Justice Department memo revealed that Khalid Sheikh Mohammed had been waterboarded 183 times. These admissions rekindled a long, ongoing debate on whether waterboarding is acceptable, legal, or even effective.

Then-president George W. Bush was on the positive side; after leaving office, he said, "Yeah, we waterboarded Khalid Sheikh Mohammed. . . . I'd do it again to save lives." In 2002 an Office of Legal Counsel memorandum concluded that waterboarding did not "cause severe pain or suffering either physically or mentally" and therefore did not constitute torture and could be used in interrogations. Vice President Dick Cheney argued that waterboarding had been "used with great discrimination by people who know what they're doing and has produced a lot of valuable information and intelligence."

In contrast, in 2003–2004, Jack Goldsmith, the head of the Office of Legal Counsel, ordered a stop to waterboarding because of serious concerns over its legality. (His order was subsequently reversed.) Senator John McCain, the 2008 Republican presidential candidate and an ex–prisoner of war, argued that "waterboarding . . . is a mock execution and thus an exquisite form of torture . . . prohibited by American laws and values."

Although most of the proponents and detractors have argued vehemently for their positions, few of them have ever experienced the feelings that accompany being waterboarded. As one of my colleagues, Loran Nordgren, has recently shown, this can make a world of difference.

The Empathy Gap

Loran and his colleagues have been investigating the "empathy gap": the fact that people who are not experiencing a visceral state can't empathize with people who are. Thus, people who are experiencing a "cool," relatively uninvolved state don't have the same information or the same insights that people who are experiencing a "hot," involved state have.

This can be critically important for leaders. Even though they may have experienced the stresses and strains of tough, uncontrollable work situations early in their careers, these memories inevitably fade. In many ways, therefore, they may not be able to fully identify with the people they lead.

In one study from Loran's research, for instance, he and his colleagues asked two groups of people to watch a video of a man who reported that he was incredibly hungry. The video showed him opening a fast-food bag and, in three and a half minutes, finishing four cheeseburgers and a large soda, eating in a way that would not endear him to anyone who appreciates good manners.

Viewers who had not eaten for some time were not as negative toward him as people who were not hungry. Even their facial expressions as they watched the video, rated by independent coders, were more positive than the faces of viewers who did not feel hunger.

In another study, Loran and his colleagues asked people to

complete a strenuous memory task that lasted twenty minutes: their task was to memorize a string of nine-digit numbers, such as 672189835, 824273194, etc. Each number string appeared for eleven seconds, after which they were supposed to "hold the numbers in their head" for seven additional seconds before they wrote them down as accurately as they could. This task was then repeated, forty times in a row.

I don't know about you but, personally, I get tired just thinking about trying to do this.

The experiment's participants then read the story of a mother who went to a grocery store to buy baby formula the morning after she had stayed up most of the night with her teething baby. When she was checking out, she realized that she was five cents short of the cost of the formula and the cashier, a member of an ethnic minority group, refused to sell it to her. The mom became agitated, screamed at the cashier, "Go back to your own country," and stomped out of the store empty-handed.

People who had completed the boring, tiring number-string task evaluated the mother significantly more positively, were more compassionate, and saw themselves as more similar to her than did people who either had done a much simpler task or had imagined doing a really fatiguing task. Thus, to empathize with someone in pain, whether from hunger or fatigue, it appears that you must be experiencing pain yourself—you can't just imagine the feeling.

Loran and his colleagues have also found that people who are fatigued are not particularly kind to impulsive eaters and people who are hungry are not particularly kind to people who act out after missing sleep. Thus they conclude that people must also have *directly related experiences* to truly feel empathy for another person. As Loran puts it, "People in one affective state cannot appreciate or predict another one." In essence, we naturally experience a gap in our ability to empathize with people who are in distress. Thus, if you haven't experienced waterboarding or other forms of torture, it is hard to imagine how painful and disturbing they are: "People cannot appreciate the severity of interrogation practices they themselves are not experiencing. By underestimating the pain of enhanced interrogation, people may perceive objectively tortuous practices to be morally or legally acceptable."

This is also particularly evident in classic psychological research on the subtly induced but unexpectedly powerful effects of imprisonment, on both the guards and the people who are imprisoned. Obviously, ethical restraints make it impossible for researchers to put undeserving volunteers into real prison conditions or to subject people to actual torture. But at Stanford University in 1971, Professor Philip Zimbardo and his students—who did not anticipate many of the outcomes that they observed—came close.

In their now-famous study, they recruited twenty-one people, mostly college students, who volunteered to be either a prisoner or a guard—they did not know which it would be—in a mock prison for $15 a day (now worth about $80). The researchers built their "prison" in the basement of the psychology department. The local police "arrested" some of the volunteers as realistically as they could by flashing the lights on their police cars, using handcuffs as they took people from their apartments, and the like.

The randomly assigned guards were issued military-style uniforms and silver reflecting sunglasses, which made it impossible to see their eyes. The prisoners wore loose smocks, no underwear, nylon stocking caps, and their prison number. They were never addressed by name and they were housed in barren cells. All of this was designed to take away their individuality.

Prior to its start, the university's Human Subjects Research Review committee reviewed and approved the research plan and all of the participants voluntarily signed a standard consent form. Everyone involved was informed about the setup in advance. No one, however, fully realized what would happen.

The results were unexpectedly and incredibly scary. People got into their roles quickly, in a big way; this was true for both prisoners and guards. As Zimbardo noted, "Our planned two-week investigation . . . had to be ended prematurely after only six days. . . . In only a few days, our guards became sadistic and our prisoners became depressed and showed signs of extreme stress." He also noted that "the power the guards assumed each time they donned these uniforms was matched by the powerlessness the prisoners felt in their wrinkled smocks. The worst abuses occurred during the night shift, when guards felt that the authorities noticed them least." In the end, the researchers became so frightened by the guards' acts of unbridled dominance—bordering on outright brutality—that they terminated the experiment.

Lord Acton's famous remark that "power tends to corrupt; absolute power corrupts absolutely" is directly applicable here. The guards had enormous power and used it, even though they had no idea beforehand that they would be guards or how those roles would affect them. Neither did the trained professional psychologists who ran the experiment.

This study is a perfect example of what can happen when we start with an empathy gap and add a powerful role (like a leader's). In fact, the empathy gap–power combination can have serious consequences in all sorts of interactions, such as masking the psychic pain and stress that so many people feel at work. In particular, leaders who are on their way up the corporate ladder are likely to have insufficient empathy for and understanding of the travails of competent individuals who, because of the narrowing opportunities for succession, get stuck at a lower level and suffer indignities, slights, and self-recrimination. It's no wonder that depression is evidencing such a dramatic increase in the United

Waterboarding and Leadership

Although waterboarding may seem distant from everyday leaders, it's an event that reveals an important, overarching issue about leadership as well as five basic problems that leaders naturally face.

The overarching issue: leaders have tremendous power. Obviously, most workplaces are not as severe as jails or prisons, and most leaders truly care about their team members. But power is seductive and immediately opens doors to corrupt and dominant behavior. In particular, when leaders impose their will, they put their team members in extremely difficult situations, often without realizing it—and this completely reverses the philosophy behind *Do Nothing!* leaders.

The first of the five basic problems that result from leaders having so much power arises because leaders (like people in general) naturally feel that they are the center of the universe. Although we don't think about this consciously, it is not surprising that this feeling can dominate and seriously influence every second of our lives: we only see through our own eyes; we don't know what an object feels like when someone else touches it; we don't know how lobster, steak, or broccoli tastes to anyone else; we don't even know if other people see blue, red, and yellow the way we see them. In other words, we experience the world in a biased, self-focused way, naturally and normally.

In a word, people tend to be decidedly and naturally *egocentric*.

The problem with egocentrism for leaders is that, even though we often think of leadership as an individual activity, it is actually a *social activity*. A particularly apt way to think of this is an old

Hopi Indian* saying: "One finger cannot lift a pebble." In essence, leaders cannot be effective on their own. If you don't think this is true, do a simple test: find an empty room somewhere, walk in, start leading, and see how effective it is.

In terms of our own leadership strategies, our natural egocentrism leads us to focus on what we do as *individual* leaders. This natural tendency means that we can make serious leadership mistakes because egocentric leaders who have a strong self-focus naturally pay less attention to their team members and more attention to themselves—even though their success depends on their team members' contributions. When leaders act egocentrically, they quickly turn their interactions into monologues rather than dialogues—and it is a rare leader who can be effective without dialogue.

This is one of the biggest hurdles that any successful leader must overcome. To be effective, leaders must get away from their natural, egocentric tendencies and focus their attention on their own team members because these are the people they need to be successful.

As we've seen, unless we directly and immediately experience another person's situation, we are prone to underestimate the demands that it places on them, as well as to underestimate the strength of their normal reactions and feelings. This tendency to experience an empathy gap is the second major problem that's embedded within the power of leadership. More generally, empathy gap research suggests that we are not particularly adept at taking other people's perspectives into account: egocentrism limits our ability to "get into someone else's shoes." This is an old, old saying, and it sounds so simple, yet it is deceptively, maddeningly difficult, for two reasons. On the one hand, we have a hard time getting out of our own shoes because we are so rooted in

* Quoted by Phil Jackson, professional basketball's most successful coach, in his wonderful book, *Sacred Hoops: Spiritual Lessons of a Hardwood Warrior.*

our own individual experience (as the center of our own universes); on the other hand, because we find it so difficult to understand exactly what someone else is experiencing, it is hard to get into other people's shoes and truly understand how they feel. Thus, leaders all too often live in their own worlds and don't fully understand the worlds of their team members and employees.

These problems do not stop with the two E's (egocentrism + the empathy gap). They get complicated by the repeated interpersonal interactions that leaders have every day.

Effective leaders need to be aware of their ultimate goals, all the time. In particular, all of their actions, throughout each day, must be designed to achieve those goals. In other words, to be successful, leaders need to be constantly thinking about how their team can take that next step, avoid that next obstacle, and constantly achieve more.

Achieving those goals, by allowing your team members to do their jobs, is critical for your success as a leader. To do this well, it pays, oddly enough, to consider an overarching leadership issue by remembering some of the lessons we learned in high school physics.

Newtonian Leadership

Newton's third law of motion states that every action has an equal and opposite reaction. This is true in the physical world because of conservation of mass and conservation of energy: any push in one direction leads to an equal and opposite push, in terms of mass and energy, in the opposite direction.

Thankfully, this is not the case for leaders and their actions: every action does *not* have an equal and opposite reaction. Life would be wildly chaotic if it did. But every leadership action does tend to lead to some kind of reaction (unless people haven't noticed what the leader has done). Again, this is natural: leaders engage in actions that they hope will have the reactions they intended.

If we take Newton's third law seriously and extend its ideas to leadership, we begin to ask some critical questions about actions and reactions. For instance, which is more important: your actions as a leader or your team's reactions to your actions?

Most astute leaders realize that their team members' reactions are far more important than their own actions. Experienced leaders can think of many examples when they thought they were doing something absolutely brilliant that (somehow) did not produce its intended effects. In other words, their strategic genius got nowhere because people did not react as they had hoped. These same leaders can also think of examples when they engaged in off-the-cuff, unplanned, less-than-ideal leadership action and, somehow or other, things worked out brilliantly. Even though their leadership actions were almost hopeless, the resulting positive outcomes made them heroes. Both of these situations indicate that team members' reactions are far more important than their leader's actions.

Unfortunately, this leads to a serious disconnect, because we naturally think most about our own actions, about what *we* are going to do. We typically focus on what we can do to achieve our ultimate goals, rather than on our team's reactions. This means that, far too often, our attention is fundamentally misdirected. Like Newton's third law, this problem is the third natural result of having power as a leader.

Rather than spending so much of our time and effort on what we will do as leaders, we need to *focus our attention, first and foremost, on the reactions that we want,* and only then think about what actions we will engage in to elicit them.

This fundamental mistake—thinking first about our own actions rather than the reactions we hope will follow—is the reason for many, if not most, of history's leadership failures.

The Leadership Law

Think of the reaction that you want first, then determine the actions you can take to maximize the chances that those reactions will actually happen

Most leaders tend to be well intentioned most of the time: they want their actions to work. When they focus on their own actions, they hope that people will not only interpret their actions positively but also that they will interpret their actions as they intended. Leaders act in hopes that their team members will react appropriately and, ultimately, approach their hoped-for results. When they pay insufficient attention to other people's likely reactions, however, they can be in for a surprise, and too often, a very painful surprise.

Imagine, for instance, that you are about to go into a negotiation that could be either cooperative or competitive. You haven't negotiated with your counterparts before, and you are afraid they might be tough. You also think that whatever they win in the negotiation you will lose. As a result, you formulate a strong, competitive strategy. What kind of reaction are you likely to generate? Almost inevitably, you will stimulate a competitive response and lose any chance of gaining the mutually cooperative benefits that might have been available—without ever knowing how they might have reacted to a more cooperative approach.

The key, overarching lesson here is so important that I call it the Leadership Law: think first of the reactions that you would like and only then think of the actions that you should take to achieve them. The Leadership Law is a subtle but critical change in the way that we think about leadership and a leader's activities. Don't think of your own actions first, even though this is so natural. Instead, to be more successful more of the time, you must make a strategic shift away from your natural tendencies so that you can consistently and repeatedly follow the Leadership Law. This small change in the way you approach your leadership responsibilities can radically alter your effectiveness, both short- and long-term.

Obviously, people are far from perfect in predicting other people's reactions: it is even difficult to predict our best friends' reactions. But it pays to try, particularly because focusing on our own actions can be so problematic.

Transparency

So far we have seen that, like anyone else, leaders naturally, implicitly act as if they are the center of their own universe; they are particularly poor at getting out of their own shoes and into other people's shoes; and they tend to focus on their own actions before they consider their team members' likely reactions. These problems extend even further because of two additional, natural tendencies: leaders tend to think that people see events and situations the way they see them, and they think that their team members will interpret their actions as they intend for them to be interpreted. In essence, because leaders see their own worlds so clearly, they often believe—or at least act like they believe—that other people see the world the same way they do.

Another of my colleagues, Vicki Medvec, with her collaborators, Tom Gilovich and Ken Savitsky, calls this "the transparency effect": people think that their friends and colleagues completely and clearly understand their ideas; they feel that they are wonderful communicators and that after they deliver a message, everybody "gets it." Thus, not only are we focused primarily on ourselves; we think that other people are focused on us, too.

Social psychologists Dale Griffin and Lee Ross presented a perfect example in one of their experiments. They asked people to use their fingers to tap the melody of a song on their desks so that a person who heard their tapping could guess the name of the song. Tappers guessed that far more listeners would guess the right song than actually did. Why do the tappers get this so wrong? As they are tapping, they hear the song in their heads. Listeners, however, have no access to this additional information— all they hear are a bunch of (hopefully) rhythmic tappings that don't add up to much.

If we think of leaders as tappers, it is pretty clear that, at least some of the time, they hear (and see) symphonies of effective, well-coordinated action. This is what they hope to accomplish— but is it what they communicate to their orchestra, their team members? Their rich visions may be radically different from the—almost necessarily—more limited messages they actually send. Even when they are aware that they have not been completely transparent, they may be so rooted in their own experience, in their own vision, that it can be particularly hard to overcome the natural communication gap that so often exists.

I have taught negotiations for more than three decades. My students are smart people who have had a lot of experience. But each time I teach a negotiations course, I have to consciously remind myself how little people know about negotiating well. Yes, they have a lot of experience, and we can think of many of their experiences as negotiations. But did they think of their experiences as negotiations? Did they analyze them carefully, before and after the event, to do as well as they could? Did they ever read a book about the theory or practice of negotiations? Obviously the answer to most of these questions is "No." This means that I have to work extremely hard to start from their perspective rather than my own, to make sure that I present exercises and lessons in my classes that *they* can relate to immediately. I don't have to start by assuming that they have absolutely zero knowledge about negotiations—but it doesn't hurt for me to think this way, because that will help me get in tune with their perceptions and their orientation rather than my own.

If we take a leader who naturally feels that his ideas and messages are transparent and we add a little power, that leader tends to think that his ideas are *even more transparent*. In other words, people who have power believe that their audiences understand their messages even more than those of people who don't have power. Assuming that your ideas are transparent and easily understood is the fourth natural problem of having power as a leader. Although we know that communication is difficult and imperfect, leaders can easily fool themselves to think that their messages have been heard, intact and unaltered, clear and complete.

This can go so far that people often believe their audiences understand and are sympathetic to their *intentions*. Thus, when a leader takes a risk by giving a young team member a challenging job, the leader often feels proud: her self-focus leads her to think that she has given someone a chance to thrive and, even though there is risk in doing this, she has done the right thing and will be appreciated for it. Team members, in contrast, are much more likely to be thinking about the benefits this new challenge might provide—*to them*. Like their leaders, team members are also egocentric, and this means that a leader's thoughts and intentions may be far less transparent than the leader thinks they are.

On a Grand Stage

These illusions can be devastating, particularly when they occur on grand stages—for instance, in the international arena.

History provides many examples when leaders' egocentrism led them to misinterpret or ignore other people's critical reactions. Leaders make so many choices that their histories are almost never singularly good or singularly bad, but some leadership choices have had amazingly serious consequences. Add to this the fact that people (and especially historians) tend to dwell on the outcomes of decisions rather than on the value of the decisions at the time a leader made them, and the problems leaders create for themselves can multiply.

Consider, for instance, the leadership history of Neville Chamberlain, a tremendously sad story. Chamberlain was the prime minister of Great Britain prior to and at the start of World War II. The events immediately preceding the war are a perfect example of some of the problems that come from having power, being egocentric, and taking a limited perspective.

In the late 1930s, with clear evidence of increasing aggression from Germany, Chamberlain and his supporters in Parliament adopted an "appeasement" plan, a strategy designed to restrict Germany's aggressive incursions while still preserving peace.

The British people still suffered from the aftereffects of World War I: they had no interest in engaging in another world war. In addition, their previous allies, Russia and Italy, had aligned with Germany, reducing the likely success of forceful resistance. Except for Winston Churchill and some of his colleagues, Chamberlain's plan had considerable support. In light of what actually happened, however, it now seems that he was overcommitted to his strategy, even when he recognized its limitations.

Chamberlain's negotiations with Hitler and Mussolini prior to the war were part of his appeasement plan. One result was Britain's formal recognition of Italy's controversial conquest of Ethiopia. Worse yet, when German forces advanced into Austria, Chamberlain acknowledged that "it is perfectly evident now that force is the only argument Germany understands." Yet after

Germany annexed Austria, Britain's only response was a strong note of protest, and Chamberlain continued to hope that negotiations would provide a peaceful solution.

In September 1938, following additional negotiations, Hitler reneged on earlier agreements and pushed to annex part of Czechoslovakia. He also expanded his demands to annex parts of Poland and Hungary as elements of his "German reunification plan."

In retrospect, it seems strange to comprehend that Chamberlain continued to negotiate with Hitler—even after Austria and his own realization that force might be needed to stop German expansion. Instead, he stuck to his appeasement plan in hopes that negotiations would contain Germany's aggression and avoid war.

Thus, after reaching an agreement with Hitler to give up part of Czechoslovakia—against the Czechs' wishes—Chamberlain had a final private conference with Hitler, at Hitler's apartment. At that meeting, Chamberlain obtained Hitler's signature on a short, three-paragraph "Anglo-German Agreement," since called the Munich Agreement, "symbolic of the desire of our two people never to go to war again."

Chamberlain left the meeting feeling absolutely triumphant: he had the paper with their signatures in his breast pocket and patted it, saying, "I've got it!" Hitler, in contrast, told one of his colleagues that same day, "That piece of paper is of no further significance whatever."

In a public statement on his return, Chamberlain told the English people, "My good friends, this is the second time there has come back from Germany to Downing Street peace with honor. I believe it is peace for our time. We thank you from the bottom of our hearts. Now I recommend you go home, and sleep quietly in your beds." King George VI concurred: "After the magnificent efforts of the Prime Minister in the cause of peace, it is my fervent hope that a new era of friendship and prosperity may be dawning among the peoples of the world."

Winston Churchill, however, told the House of Commons that "England has been offered a choice between war and shame. She has chosen shame, and will get war."

Although we all know the ultimate outcome, and hindsight is an unfair judge, Chamberlain acted, even after repeated evidence to the contrary, as if his counterpart, Hitler, viewed their agreement as he did. He truly believed that their agreement would preserve peace for the people of England and for all of Europe. Instead, it is clear that Hitler had an entirely different view.

We can surmise (again, because we have the unfair advantage of knowing the outcome) that Chamberlain should have understood how different Hitler's viewpoint was from his own. As it happened, either country had the power to embark on a warlike strategy that the other could not prevent. In this case, Hitler and Germany were the aggressors and, even though Chamberlain recognized and acknowledged the signs, he still stuck to his original policy, and may have been blinded by it, even as evidence continued to accumulate that it was foolhardy.

As a result, England found itself much less prepared than it might otherwise have been as hostilities escalated. On March 15, 1939, Germany invaded the Czech provinces of Bohemia and Moravia, including Prague, and on April 7, Italy invaded Albania. On August 23, Chamberlain wrote to Hitler to make it clear that Britain would fulfill its obligations and defend Poland; Hitler responded by preparing for an invasion, saying, "Our enemies are small worms. I saw them at Munich."

It is hard to imagine a more serious misinterpretation of a critical counterpart's intentions. It appears that Chamberlain was simply unable to walk in Hitler's shoes, to take his point of view, or to understand how he truly felt. Worse yet, Chamberlain's appeasement plan was so important to him that he acted as if Hitler understood and agreed with it. As a result, his natural inclinations blocked his ability to see the truly harsh reality that confronted him and his people.

A Final Step over the Cliff

Leaders are egocentric, they lack empathy, they naturally focus on their own actions first, and they often think that people understand them completely. These four problems are magnified even further because we also tend to have another natural failing: we are not particularly adept at understanding how our own behaviors influence the unfolding process of our interactions.

During real-time interchanges of word, action, and reaction, for instance, our initial actions can be incredibly potent, even though we often don't realize it. If, as noted, we begin a negotiation by being competitive, our counterparts are likely to respond in kind. We can then (egocentrically) view them as being much more competitive than we were in our initial actions (which we might not see as being so competitive in the first place). By misperceiving the impact of our own initial actions, we can seriously misinterpret our counterparts' actions—all without being aware of our own impact—and this can seriously bias our evaluations of them.

Karl Weick, a famous organizational psychologist at the University of Michigan, often refers to one-on-one interactions in the workplace as "double-interacts": one person's actions stimulate natural responses which then stimulate additional natural responses, all within a confined interpersonal space. Thus, double-interacts can expand to become triple-interacts when the first actors, in our case leaders, may not realize that they have had such a big influence on a second person's actions, and then they react strongly themselves. Some of those strong reactions tend to be internal and evaluative: leaders are always judging their team members and making conclusions based on their team members' actions. Sadly, what leaders often leave out of this process is the potent impact of their own initial actions.

Psychologists think about these kinds of events in another way when they talk about the "fundamental attribution error": the tendency to attribute causal influence to people even when the situation has a lot to do with their actions. In the case of leader–team member interactions, leaders often attribute causal force to their team members, even when the leaders themselves have had a lot to do in determining their team members' actions. In other words, leaders often create situations and then blame their team members for performing poorly within them—without realizing that they were at fault in the first place.

Thus, leaders who have not taken the time to get to know their team members well or who violate the Leadership Law by focusing on their own actions rather than emphasizing their team members' reactions often make a host of different mistakes that they never take credit for. Here are some examples:

- A leader buys a team member a lovely bottle of wine for his tenth wedding anniversary without realizing that his team member's wife is a recovering alcoholic; the leader is disappointed when his team member does not seem particularly appreciative or grateful.
- A leader promotes her top employee to a new management position without providing the employee with any managerial or leadership training. The employee may have seemed immensely mature and truly talented at her previous job, but may not know how to handle subtle leadership challenges. The leader then concludes that

this employee really doesn't have leadership potential after all.

- After a practice talk, a speech coach asks the speaker, "When during your speech did you feel most confident?" A second coach asks, "When during your speech did you feel least confident?" It is no surprise that the second coach gives *the same speech* a lower grade than the first coach does.

These are just three of many possible examples. Each includes an element of the five natural problems that individuals have as leaders.

Five Natural Problems of Individuals as Leaders

This fifth interaction problem also results because people's expectations lead them to act in ways that stimulate behavior that they can then interpret as confirming their expectations, that is, self-fulfilling prophecies, which resemble the negative version of the Pygmalion effect—expecting something awful and getting it—that we discussed in the last chapter.

In essence, first impressions can encourage leaders to form expectations about other people's abilities and characteristics that the leader's subsequent actions then facilitate. Thus, as one example, when very young couples eat at nice restaurants, servers and maître d's often expect them to leave small tips; this expectation leads them to give young couples poor tables and less attentive service, which in turn leads young couples who might otherwise leave a good tip to leave a small one instead. Similarly, leaders who expect that their female team members will be less effective at quantitative tasks might still give them quantitative tasks; by indicating, explicitly or implicitly, that they don't expect

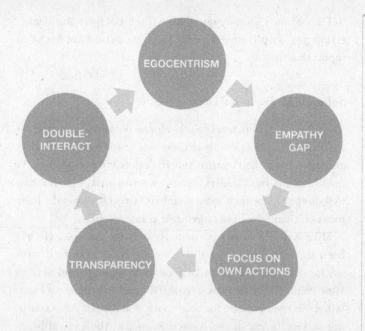

high performance, they create a stereotype threat that can make women more anxious about their performance, which in turn can lead them to perform more poorly than they otherwise would. In other words, not only do we often find what we are looking for in people, we sometimes *create* what we are looking for in people. In this last example, the end result can be a person who is actually quite skilled at math beginning to think that she is not, leading her to avoid quantitative tasks, and ultimately causing her potential skills to deteriorate.

Karl Weick has frequently analyzed situations like this, in which small actions amplify interactions that then lead to larger and larger consequences. When these kinds of patterns repeat themselves, leaders can find that far too many of their seemingly subtle, initial actions ultimately have huge effects, and not always to their liking.

The obvious follow-up question to this list of five natural leadership problems is whether easy antidotes exist. I am happy to report that they do.

Solution #1: Focus on Them

The first major, unnatural solution for leaders is to shift their focus, to start thinking less about their own desires and perspectives and more about their team members' desires and perspectives. As mature adults, most leaders know themselves pretty well. But how well do they know their team members? Great leaders take their focus off themselves and target their team members.

Mike Krzyzewski is a particularly striking example. He has been an exceedingly successful basketball coach at Duke University for over thirty years. Mike grew up in Chicago and went to West Point, where he played basketball and was the team's captain in his senior season for head coach Bob Knight. After coaching service teams in the Armed Forces, at the U.S. Military Academy Prep School, and at West Point, he became head coach at Duke in 1980.

His success there has been nothing short of phenomenal. "Coach K" has led his teams to four NCAA championships, eleven Final Fours, twelve ACC regular season titles, and thirteen ACC championships. He is the head coach of the U.S. men's national basketball team, which won the gold medal at the 2008 Summer Olympics and the 2010 World Championships, and he's in the Naismith Memorial Basketball Hall of Fame.

He has also written his own book on leadership, which gives us direct insights into many of the reasons for his continued, consistent success. One of his most notable strategies is that he asks questions, lots of questions.

This sounds so simple, doesn't it? But think what this does—first and foremost, it focuses his attention on his players. Although he spends a lot of time watching them play and determining their various competencies, he also asks them if they want to guard their opponent's best shooter; if they are as comfortable dribbling with their left hand as their right; and if they want to take the last shot in a close game. (This is just the tip of the iceberg. He asks them many, many more questions.)

By asking questions, he gets three immediate benefits: he conveys respect, he builds trust, and he gets information. All three help him build a set of strategies that fit his current team, their skills, and their preferences.

Asking questions also moves the focus away from him and toward his team members. For a leader with such sterling credentials, it's also pretty ironic. He is one of the most successful basketball coaches of all time, someone who knows as much about the game as anyone alive, and who are the targets of his questions? Eighteen- and nineteen-year-old kids. This is not only amazing, it's also amazingly effective.

Solution #2: Learn to Take Your Team Members' Perspectives

Leadership positions almost always come with power, which can be a real problem. Our own research suggests that it can be particularly problematic for people who have just moved into a powerful position, for example, people who have just been promoted to be leaders.

Another of my colleagues, Adam Galinsky, has done a ton of research on the effects of perspective taking and power. It turns out that people who feel that they have power—they don't actually have to be powerful, they just have to *feel powerful*—are horrible at understanding other people's feelings.

In many of their studies, Adam and his colleagues randomly assign two groups of people to different tasks. The first group writes about a time when they felt they had power over someone; the second group writes about a time when they felt someone had power over them. This leads to two distinct groups: one that feels powerful and one that doesn't. In one study, Adam and his colleagues asked each of the participants to look at a series of twenty-four photographs of people's faces; in each picture, the person was expressing happiness, fear, anger, or sadness.

Their task was to guess which of the four emotions the pictured person was feeling. As in many previous studies, women were better at this task than men: they are far superior to men on all sorts of interpersonal dimensions, including empathy and detecting other people's feelings. More important for Adam's research, the people who felt powerful made almost 50 percent more errors than the people who did not. Thus, not only are people fairly poor at detecting other people's feelings, they are even worse at it when they feel powerful.

The same kinds of errors show up in many other situations. An international group of researchers, for instance, asked people to have a face-to-face conversation in which they and their counterparts would reveal personal experiences that had caused them suffering. People who felt powerful reported less distress and less compassion when they heard about their conversation partners' suffering than people who did not feel powerful. The emotions of the people who felt powerful were even reflected in their electrocardiograms. The clear conclusion: people who felt powerful were less motivated to invest emotionally in their conversation partners and less motivated to get to know them. It was as if they didn't *need* the other person because they felt they were doing quite well by themselves. Clearly, these can be dangerous, but all too natural, feelings for leaders.

It is not surprising that leaders can be remarkably inept at taking other people's perspectives into account. A conscious push, however, can have a tremendously positive effect. Take, for example, a study of student doctors. Prior to their third-year exam, which tests them on history taking, physicals, and patient communication, some students were told, "When you see your patient, imagine what the patient is experiencing as if you were that person, looking at the world through the patient's eyes and walking through the world in the patient's shoes." They were also told to write a brief note (ten lines or fewer) about each case, describing what they imagined the patient was experiencing.

After they had finished their rounds, the patients rated the student doctors on their listening skills, caring, fostering participation in the patient's care, trust, and the patient's overall satisfaction. The patients whose med student visitors had experienced the perspective-taking intervention were significantly more satisfied than patients whose visitors had not experienced the intervention. This kind of study shows that reminding people that it pays to take others' perspectives can help, a lot.

Solution #3: Follow the Leadership Law

Avoid thinking of your own actions first; instead think of the reactions you would like to see from your team members. Only after you have identified your hoped-for outcomes should you start thinking about how you can mold your own actions to achieve them.

Solutions to the Natural Problems of Individuals as Leaders

As we've seen, Neville Chamberlain is a particularly sad example of someone who failed to follow the Leadership Law. Another is Michael Brown, who was the director of the Federal Emergency Management Agency (FEMA) when Hurricane Katrina

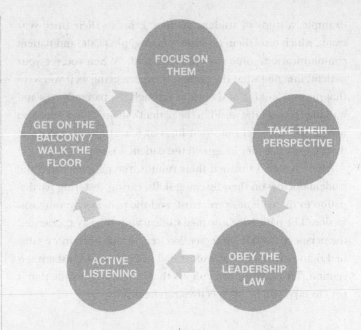

devastated New Orleans and the Gulf Coast. Much has been written about the government's mismanagement of this disaster. Michael Brown was the federal government's point person—the one individual who was most responsible for bringing outside help to New Orleans and the Gulf Coast. Understandably, he was a central target for blame.

Many of the e-mails that he sent during the aftermath of the storm were released publicly, leading to a rash of negative reactions. For instance, on the day that Katrina struck New Orleans, Brown wrote to his deputy director of public affairs, "Can I quit now? Can I come home?" Maybe he meant this to be a joke, but at such a critical time, its release led to harsh criticisms. Two days after the storm hit, one of FEMA's few employees in New Orleans wrote to Brown that "the situation is past critical," noting that many people were near death and they were running out of food and water at the Superdome. Brown's entire response was: "Thanks for the update. Anything specific I need to do or tweak?" In a third e-mail, a couple days later, he wrote to an acquaintance, "I'm trapped now, please rescue me."

Not all of us expect that our e-mails will be made public. But leaders in positions of authority, in critical times, are almost always evaluated carefully. As James Joyce noted, "Mistakes are the portals of discovery." Certainly every leader makes mistakes, but many mistakes are avoidable if leaders first consider how other people will react to their actions. Had Neville Chamberlain or Michael Brown focused more on the likely reactions—by Hitler, in Chamberlain's case, and by the general public in Brown's—they might have taken much more positive, more effective actions. They didn't practice the Leadership Law.

When you do consider other people's likely reactions, you will not always be successful: people are only moderately accurate in their attempts to predict other people's behaviors. But if you adopt better interpersonal predictions as your goal, you will be motivated to learn more about your team members so that you can structure situations to give them the chance to willingly and confidently display their abilities (à la Mike Krzyzewski). In other words, by trying to understand how to prompt positive reactions, you can begin to use self-fulfilling prophecies and the high expectations of the Pygmalion effect to create constructive situations that will increase the likelihood that your team members will succeed.

Solution #4: Active Listening

Active listening is an old leadership communication technique that gets too little play these days, and not for any good reason. Management scholars still talk about listening skills, but they rarely talk about active listening. Carl Rogers, a renowned psychologist and the father of person-centered therapy, designed this technique. Active listening is a simple way to ensure constructive, substantive dialogue. It means that, when leaders tell a team member about a job they would like done, they should then ask their team member to "tell me what I just told you." The team member then describes the job in their own words. Both people then take turns speaking, with the leader providing further explanation and the team member reiterating what they have heard. When the job is complex or people conflict—situations in which misunderstandings are common—a repeated interchange helps them make sure they both understand the job and each other.

The beauty of active listening is that it helps overcome the fact that leaders and team members, like any other pair of people, are not always perfect communicators or perfect listeners: either or both of them may be distracted, half listening, or thinking about something else. Also, if there is any tension between them, they may be focused on getting ready for an argument, thinking about how they can win it rather than listening carefully.

Active listening encourages listeners to pay attention so they can repeat, in their own words, what the speaker has just said. It also encourages speakers to be clear and complete so they can limit the number of their back-and-forth exchanges. The two communicators do not need to agree on the importance of a particular job; they just have to understand it and know they both understand it.

Active listening has several benefits: it encourages leaders to think about how their team members can best hear their ideas, it pushes both people to listen carefully, and it helps avoid misunderstandings. In the end, it's easy, it's effective, and team members can use it with leaders as well as leaders using it with their team members to make sure that critical information is clearly communicated to everyone.

Solution #5: Get on the Balcony/Walk the Floor

This solution seems to be telling you to be in two places at the same time. But it does not depend on the smoke and mirrors of a magic trick: one act is metaphorical (Get on the balcony) and one is physical (Walk the floor).

William Ury has been studying and writing about negotiations for a long time. He and his colleague Roger Fisher wrote the landmark book *Getting to Yes,* which showed people that negotiations do not always have to be contentious; instead, they can be cooperative and oriented toward problem solving rather than direct conflict. Their book continues to be a big seller more than thirty years after its original publication.

Ury also wrote *Getting Past No,* which discusses the wonderful concept of "getting on the balcony," that is, acting as if you are standing on a balcony above your current situation and watching how everything unfolds—including seeing yourself in the action, at that moment. This kind of "mental distancing" helps leaders get a more objective sense of themselves and their team's interactions so that they can orchestrate future actions, especially their own, more effectively.

The balcony is an almost perfect place to observe your team: it is close enough to the action for you to see the details of what is going on but far enough away to allow you to be a bit more objective about what's happening. Although it is a metaphorical rather than literal concept, some teams use it literally: assistant coaches do this during football games when they sit in the press box, high above the field. There they can watch the entire pattern of their team's behaviors, as well as their opponents'. They remain in constant contact with the head coach so they can relay both observations and creative ideas for immediate implementation. Their eagle's eye view let's them see what the head coach, who is on the sidelines close to the action, can't.

CEOs often have their own sets of assistant coaches who sit on the balcony and observe a company's interactions. Far too many CEOs, however, combine this with staying away from the fray, keeping a distance that makes it difficult for them to get a feel for the everyday events in their organizations. This is why the first rule for a CEO has always been "Walk the floor," and it is the second half of solution #5.

CEOs often self-define their jobs as primarily involving external relations, such as attending to customers. This is clearly an important part of a CEO's job, as it is impossible to succeed without customers. But it is also difficult to succeed if an organization's internal structure is not effective. Legendary leaders like Herb Kelleher, the founder of Southwest Airlines, have been widely admired, and not just for their success; they've also been widely admired by their employees. In fact, it's not a stretch to suggest that Kelleher and Southwest's success resulted, at least in part, because he knew everyone at Southwest's headquarters by name. They all felt that he genuinely cared about them. This kind of personal attention is almost certain to generate a positive reaction, including greater commitment to the firm, which is exactly what every CEO hopes to achieve.

Michael Abrashoff, the amazingly successful captain of the USS *Benfold* and the author of *It's Your Ship*, is another great example of walking the floor—except in his case, it was walking the deck. At the time of its construction, the *Benfold* was one of the most sophisticated and technologically advanced ships in the U.S. Navy. Sadly, when Abrashoff took over as its captain, it was also the Navy's worst-rated ship. The Navy takes great care in evaluating its ships, their personnel, and their performance. Morale and retention among the *Benfold*'s 310 sailors were huge problems when Abrashoff took over: the sailors acted as if they didn't respect their previous captain, their performance on all sorts of tests was substandard, and it seemed as if they couldn't wait to get out of the Navy. They were not motivated to perform and, not surprisingly, their performance as a combat unit was abysmal. Within seven months, however, they received the Spokane Trophy for being the best ship in the Pacific Fleet.

When Abrashoff· became the *Benfold*'s captain, he made it a point to walk the deck every day. Any time he encountered a sailor who had gone beyond the call of duty, he would pin a medal on him, on the spot. (He figured he could fill the paperwork out later.) Also, anytime someone told him about a sailor doing something heroic, he sought that sailor out and pinned a medal on him, too.

Unlike the gold stars we got in school, military medals endure, both substantively and in a sailor's mind. They provide a clear and important symbol of excellent performance that sailors get to wear every time they put on their dress uniforms.

Public recognition of excellent performance is a great way to stimulate motivation, and that is exactly what happened on the *Benfold*. The Navy had a policy that a ship's captain could award a total of 15 medals a year. In his first year as captain, Abrashoff awarded 150. (He figured that the Navy would not keep track of how many medals he was ordering.) One of the many positive results was that the ship's reenlistment rate went from a dismal 28 percent when he took over to 99 percent two years later. Not only that, his sailors were constantly suggesting new and better ways to perform their jobs, at less cost. As each of them grew into their roles, the captain's responsibilities diminished, and Abrashoff could do less and less.

The Plan

It's time for another dream. Once again, you have just returned from vacation. (You may have left your cell phone at home while you were gone.) Once again, you have gone into the office early to try to catch up.

As you are familiarizing yourself with your team's current situation, your team members start drifting by your open door. They each stop to chat, and then they all go to their jobs and do 120 percent of what you had hoped for and expected of them that day. Then they do it again, and again. They never interrupt you or ask you for help or bring you a problem. They just get to work on time and do more than you expected, each and every day.

Another nice dream, isn't it? But alas, it is a dream. Your team members are not robots, so they can't be this well programmed. Instead they are normal human beings, hopefully with a good bit of talent and conscientiousness.

You and every other leader in the world are also normal human beings. As a result, you have all of the natural tendencies of any other human being. (This is not to say that you don't also have a large number of good qualities, too.) You are at least a little bit egocentric; you may have missed some of the nuances of one of your team member's perspectives during an important recent interaction; you often focus on what you need to do next; you believe that you are a better communicator than your team members do; and you rarely recognize how you have acted as a stimulus that has activated a response you're not happy about. These are all natural, normal human actions. Leaders are not immune: they have all of the natural tendencies that other people do.

In addition, most leaders want to get better. This chapter gives you five direction plans. Although they sound simple, and they can be simple, they require that you overcome your natural tendencies. But even a few steps in the right direction will yield potent returns. Here they are, one more time.

First, focus on them, not on you. The "them" in this equation is everyone you interact with: your team members, your customers, your suppliers, your bosses, your consultants. Follow the first rule of sales: determine what your customers need and see if you can provide it for them. We are all in sales, and all of us can get better at it with a little attention and effort if we focus more on them than on ourselves.

Second, get out of your own shoes. A well-known scholar in our field has a reputation for taking his shoes off and walking around a seminar room whenever he gives a research talk. He gets out of his shoes—literally. I can't help thinking that this allows him to appreciate his audience's perspectives; maybe it helps him to be more comfortable and relaxed, too. Either way, he gives great talks and he connects with his audience beautifully.

Third, be a social psychologist: don't just try to understand people's behavior after you've observed it—actually try to predict it. You can only really understand a phenomenon, scientifically, if you can predict when it will happen and when it won't. Social psychologists try to do this all the time. Even though they spend their careers observing and analyzing normal, everyday behavior, they don't always get it right. But their quest is illuminating and, over time, the field of social psychology has provided all sorts of insights into why people behave the way they do. As a social psychologist myself, I could not have written this book ten years ago, probably not even five. We've learned an enormous amount in the last few years, and I hope to continue to enrich the rest of this book with some of social psychology's insights. Also, all of us are amateur social psychologists anyway, so the lack of a PhD should not stop you from making predictions about people's reactions— before you act.

Fourth, don't just listen, listen actively. "Let me try to tell you what I just heard. I want to make sure I got it right." This is a simple script that you can use to respond to important messages that come your way during your everyday work; it is also something that you can ask of your team members. Obviously you don't want to overdo it: it's best to save active listening for important exchanges of information. The beauty of active listening is that it gets everyone on the same page—or at least a lot closer to it than they were before.

Finally, act like a mini-CEO: get on the balcony and walk the floor. (Can you do this simultaneously? Absolutely. The mind and the body of a leader don't need to be in the same place!) Know what's going on but *don't do anything*—just walk and talk and look and listen. Be involved. Care for people. And push yourself to follow the Leadership Law: take the time to think about what reactions you'd like to see next, before you act.

3

Start at the End

DURING YOUR CAREER, have you ever had a supervisor single you out, in public, and say, "For this next task, I want you to take over. You are the expert on this job. I want you to be in charge. I'll get out of the way"? I have asked this question of many, many executives. The response is far from unanimous—typically only about 10 to 20 percent raise their hands. I always choose one exec randomly and ask, "How does it feel when this happens?" The most frequent response is a simple "Good." Some people note that it's also a bit scary, as they realize they now have much more responsibility than they did just a short minute ago.[*]

People's overwhelming, primary reaction, however, particularly after they have gotten into the job, is not just to feel good but to feel great about themselves because the boss has just recognized them for their skills, publicly, and has given them the authority

---

[*] Note: some team members are shy and freeze in these situations. A great leader will realize this and let the shy person know, in advance, that this is going to happen at their next meeting. This way it will be neither a shock nor a surprise.

and the discretion to use those skills and show them off—to their team members, to their customers, and to other members of the organization. The boss has shined a spotlight on them and recognized them for what they can do; on top of that, they get the authority to do the job and lead. The immediate result: *people feel taller*. Their leader has given them pride, and the positive feelings that this creates are not momentary—they last for a long time.

Pride is a huge motivator: when people feel proud of what they can do and they have a chance to do it, and be recognized and rewarded for it, they are almost always highly motivated to perform. This leads to a simple moral: *leaders don't do this often enough*. To be honest, I have no idea why they don't, because it is good for everyone: it is great for the people who have just been singled out and given the authority to exercise their skills, it allows their leaders to move closer to doing absolutely nothing, and the targeted person's performance tends to increase as well.

It also affects other team members, who tend to have one of two reactions: they either feel slighted or they feel motivated to show off their skills and achieve more, too, so they can take charge and lead their own part of the team's projects. People who feel slighted need to get over these kinds of unproductive feelings. Obviously, any of a team's members can sulk and stall the work flow, but all this accomplishes is to make them unhappy and put a stain on their reputation. Instead, they need to realize that mimicking the chosen few will serve them far better. This will fulfill the goals of a consistent, transparent meritocracy that encourages team members to recognize and respond to its incentives. This kind of system can work particularly well because every team member needs to act like a leader (when leadership is necessary) and every leader (except, possibly, the CEO) is part of a team. By giving people a chance to show off what they can do, great leaders help grow new leaders and their entire team benefits, individually and collectively.

Transactive Memory

If you can lead more effectively by singling out one person to take over a job, why not single out two? Or three? Or more? The logic of this tactic does not need to stop with one person. It only needs to stop when a team member's skills are insufficient for the job.

This means that it is critical for you to know your team members' skill sets; it helps even more if *everyone* on the team is aware of one another's talents. An ideal situation emerges when each member of a team has skills that, collectively, cover all of the roles that need to be fulfilled successfully to complete your current tasks, *and* you and each of your team members are all informed about each person's skill set. This sounds simple enough; it is particularly simple when your team's tasks don't change much. The results of this kind of process are particularly clear in moviemaking.

Although movie crews include a long list of critical roles, the director—the big leader—often doesn't need to discuss who is going to do what, even when the team members haven't worked together before. Instead, everyone realizes that everyone has specific skills and that each of the people in major roles will take the lead within their own realm: the location manager will identify and arrange for clearances for the locations where they will film; the cinematographer will be in charge of the filming itself; the production designer will make sure that the physical space has the right look; the props master will make sure that they have the right cars, costumes, and accessories at hand; and the editor will collect all of the film and cut it to determine how the movie will ultimately flow from one scene to the next. Successful directors often work with many of the same people repeatedly, as this gives them even more confidence that everyone can fulfill their roles. In the end, the director must be *the* person who has an overall sense of what is needed to make the movie great. As a result, she must make each of the final, critical decisions that will make that happen. To do this well, she must also know what people can and can't do so that she can orchestrate the process and help facilitate everyone's combined contributions.

Having clear expectations of one another makes it easier to adjust to a world that is rapidly changing. Thus, to be continuously effective, you must also be prepared to lead your team on all sorts of potentially unexpected jobs. This means that you need to know much more about your team members' skills than you might think. In particular, you will want to know about all sorts of seemingly irrelevant skills that your team members possess—just in case you need them.

If all of your team members also know one another's skill sets, they can be incredibly efficient in coordinating themselves when new tasks appear. This kind of shared know-how is what Daniel Wegner, a social psychologist at Harvard, calls *transactive memory:* it allows you and your team members to quickly turn to the right person when a novel task emerges. This takes the standard notion of the effectiveness of division of labor to new heights, as it helps groups cope with unexpected events and unforeseen tasks. It also explains why, in sports, teams that have played together longer tend to be more successful.

These effects are nicely documented in a study of fifty-seven Australian loan officers who were given three years of financial data for each of thirty-nine companies and were asked to predict, first on their own and then in three-person teams, which companies would go bankrupt. Some of the teams had been working together for some time; others were put together for just this task.

The results indicated that experience working together did not have much impact (although it does in many other studies). Instead, the teams that did best benefited from transactive memory and diversity: they had a diverse range of commonly known skill sets that allowed everyone to easily identify which team member was best equipped to make the prediction for each particular company. In contrast, when the team members' skills were less diverse, it was less clear who would be the best predictor, and these teams were less effective.

These findings are another indication that, by appreciating and incorporating diversity within your team, you can help it perform better. Add a bit of knowledge about your team members' usable knowledge—that is, not just what they say they can do but also what they actually can do—as well as mutual trust, and you and your team will be particularly well equipped to handle unexpected tasks. Thus, having individuals on your team who are personable, quantitative, perceptive, analytical, quick-witted, and calm, as well as being fluent in ten different languages, knowledgeable about seemingly irrelevant trivia, physically strong or fast, and both short and tall increases each person's value to the team, even if these particular skill sets or characteristics are not currently needed. Including people with extra skills broadens your team's value by increasing its range of possible successes—and retains your ability to *Do Nothing!*—even when things change.

Like many great leaders, you can achieve these performance peaks by being skilled at creating critical roles for each of your team members and making sure they understand them. This was one of the key elements in Phil Jackson's success as a coach of the Chicago Bulls and the Los Angeles Lakers. In Chicago, his team's two superstars were Michael Jordan and Scottie Pippen; their skills sets were astonishing. Because basketball is a game that pits five players from one team against five players on the other team, however, Jordan and Pippen needed their teammates' help to win.

Although Jordan and Pippen were so talented that they could do just about anything they wanted to do on a basketball court, they still had roles: Jordan's primary role was to score and

60 Pippen's primary role was to coordinate the entire team's play. Their teammates included a cast of characters who were sometimes called the "Jordanaires." In fact, they were a group of extraordinary role players who knew their roles and filled them. In the Bulls' first three championships, for instance, Horace Grant was the player who did the heavy lifting—the rebounding and interior defense—and John Paxson was their deadeye shooter; in their last three championships, Dennis Rodman was the heavy lifter and Steve Kerr was the deadeye shooter. Other players also had their own critical roles.

The key for great leaders is to construct a team that has all of the skills they need to counteract any obstacle that might come up. In sports, opposing teams are always trying to create these kinds of obstacles; many businesses use the same strategy. In the case of the Chicago Bulls, each player had his role and, as a team, they worked on building transactive memory: it was critical for everyone to know what the others' roles and skills were. They also needed to trust in one another and to restrain themselves from going beyond their specific roles.

The egocentrism of the players, however, sometimes interfered. Paxson and Kerr realized that, because of their size and (lack of) leaping ability, they could never be great rebounders. The heavy lifters, however, often wanted a bit more limelight. Dennis Rodman, for instance, sometimes wanted to move beyond his role as a defender and rebounder to be a scorer. In particular, he often seemed to be enamored of three-point shooting.

He was not a good shooter, however, and for the most part he restrained himself: in his three championship seasons with the Bulls, he took fewer than five shots a game, with only a small percentage of them being three-point shots. A problem arose, however, usually early in a game, when he would launch a three-point shot and it went in. Although his success rate was less than

DO NOTHING!

25 percent, hitting a three-pointer seemed to increase his confidence and encourage him to act as if he were a stellar shooter. This would almost inevitably lead to a string of inappropriate shots and consecutive misses, leading Phil Jackson to take him out of the game and remind him of his role: to focus on rebounding and defense rather than shooting.

This is one of those rare instances where great leaders must actually do something: when your team members' egos get the best of them and they think they can do more than they actually can, you must actively, if diplomatically and privately, restrain them.

Another moral to this story is that *unassigned roles are typically unfulfilled*. Thus, leaders must be sure to assign all of the necessary roles to someone on the team, so that each team member can fulfill their role, and so everyone accepts and is committed to fulfilling them. Teams that include people who know what they are supposed to do, who are happy to do what they are supposed to do, and who can do what they are supposed to do are successful teams. This is another way that leaders can ultimately move toward Doing Nothing. But they must also do a bit of orchestration to ensure that all of the critical roles are identified, assigned, filled, and fulfilled.

When everyone has a place, knows their place, knows their team members' places, has a wide array of skills and knowledge, and everyone believes in and satisfies one another's expectations, a team can achieve its central goals. It can also revise and increase them so they can achieve even more.

They will also enjoy one more, often unexpected benefit: when teams know that they have the skills to handle a wide array of challenges, they feel better about themselves and more connected to one another. In other words, they build a positive esprit de corps, a collective confidence that helps them perform more effectively on their everyday, nonextraordinary jobs, on their own.

If you are the only person in your team who is aware

of everyone's skill sets, you can act as the central facilitator that everyone in the team needs—and, as with brilliant movie directors, this is the perfect role for a leader who does nothing. Team members should be able to use their leaders in much the same way that they use the Internet: they don't have to know everything themselves, but if they have a source to consult to get the information they need, as well as critical skills, everyone is good to go.

The conclusions here are simple: determine who has what skills, and to what degree. Let people in your team know about one another's skill sets so they can call on them whenever they need to. Encourage your team members to expand the range of their expertise, and update your team members' inventories of each of their expanding skill sets as they do. In particular, be sure to develop the abilities that you believe your team might actually need. Then, most important of all, let individuals who can do a job do it.

No leader can do everything: as noted, one finger cannot lift a pebble. A group can't lift a pebble either unless they have the relevant skills among them and can coordinate themselves effectively, when it's necessary. At the same time, you must always keep in mind the goals that you hope to accomplish.

Goals

Most leaders have incredibly busy days, being pushed and pulled in various directions and wishing they could slow down the clock so they could get everything done. Sound familiar?

One of the natural results of this normal, hectic pace is that leaders often get so distracted that they lose sight of their ultimate goals. It is all too easy to let your immediate problems dominate your attention, to the point where you might not realize that finding the solution to some of your problems may not really help you much in getting where you want to be. Leaders need to keep a singular focus, each and every day, on their ultimate goals; they need to keep them at the front of their minds as they choose their actions and strategies. This seems so obvious but, at the same time, incredibly busy days when people are constantly asking for your attention make it easy to lose a central, goal-oriented focus. Thus, even something as simple as putting a Post-it note that describes your ultimate goals on the corner of your computer screen can help you keep focused and slow you down so that you can facilitate and orchestrate your team's actions directly toward your ultimate goal.

Here's a simple example. For many years, General Electric has had the goal of being number one or two in everything they do. This is a clear and simple goal. But do all of GE's leaders keep it in mind as they go through their everyday activities? How does this explain the fact, for instance, that after purchasing Kidder, Peabody & Co., a securities firm, in 1986, it took GE eight years to sell it, even though they experienced serious financial losses? Even a well-formulated, well-stated goal like GE's can get lost, easily, in the hectic shuffle of everyday action.

To be effective, your team's goals need to be measurable, schedulable, and accountable. If you can't measure them, you can't know whether your team has achieved them; if they aren't schedulable, you may keep putting off your ultimate evaluations to the point where you never evaluate your progress; and if no one is directly accountable, everyone might think that it's someone else's job to achieve them. Once again, a little orchestration can help you make sure that everyone is doing their jobs as well as they can. This may seem like you are actually doing something, but your team members are the ones who are actually doing the work. You should continue to wave your metaphorical conductor's wand.

This is the tangible part of effective team goals. It is also critical that your ultimate goals be aspirational: if you aren't trying to achieve more, you will not get better and your competitors will soon overtake you. Leaders must strike a fine balance between their aspirations and the goals that their team members see as achievable. Well-formulated team goals should be currently out of reach, but not ultimately out of reach.

Great leaders are also aware that, within teams, they always have three kinds of goals: superordinate, team, and individual. Team and individual goals are fairly obvious. Superordinate goals encompass the big picture: why does your team exist? Why does your company exist? What good are you doing for humanity?

Almost every company does something positive for the world: it provides a worthwhile service or makes a product that makes people's lives easier. You need to be tuned into your firm's superordinate goals, not just because these are goals that you want to achieve, but also because being constantly aware of them can help you remind your team members of them. Leaders don't do this naturally; instead, they (1) rarely pay much attention to their firm's superordinate goals, and/or (2) don't mention them very often, even though these kinds of messages can be truly inspiring.

Imagine for a minute that you are a leader in health care or education. Your superordinate goals are obvious, important, and laudable: you are working to improve people's lives by helping them to be healthier or more knowledgeable.

The tough part here is to remember how effective it can be to remind your team members that this is why you are all doing what you do. It is far too easy, for example, for middle-school principals to focus on simply surviving each day's hectic pace. This narrow focus on the here-and-now, on the immediate problems of the day, naturally leads to overmanaging. Instead, it is far better to take the time to tell a story now and then about some of their school's past successes, for example, about the recalcitrant preteenager who went on to academic success and a big, important job, or about the dyslexic student who had trouble with almost every single class until he took Mandarin and found his passion—in part because his dyslexia did not impede his ability to learn Chinese. These kinds of stories help leaders inspire their team members by reminding them of the greater good they are all doing. They also signal to the team that *you* are inspired by the organization's superordinate goals, which makes you a much better role model, too.

Remembering your superordinate goals is particularly helpful when you and your team have the unenviable task of doing *dirty work*. Chapter 1 defined dirty work as any job that no one wants to do; it also noted that every team has dirty work and that, although these are jobs that everyone hopes someone else will do, they are often essential for success. How can you help your team members do dirty work and do it well? In addition to the rotation scheme suggested in chapter 1, it helps to remind people of your superordinate goals—that way doing dirty work for a larger goal becomes a bit easier.

Another example from the Chicago Bulls shows how this works. As noted, the heavy lifter in their first three championship teams—the person who was most responsible for the team's dirty work—was a wonderful player named Horace Grant. Horace was a powerful rebounder and a smart, active defender; he was named to the NBA's All-Defensive team four times.

Horace was so good at doing the dirty work that, late in his career, Phil Jackson encouraged the Lakers to sign him for his thirteenth season, with a boost in salary. (Horace's salary peaked in his ninth season and had then started to decline.) The Lakers won a championship that year. In addition, after his fifteenth season, even though Horace had announced that he was retiring, Jackson lured him back to the Lakers again, for one more season and one more chance at a championship. In other words, after doing the dirty work for the Bulls' first three championship seasons, Horace reaped some significant rewards from his old coach, late in his career.

The combined successes of Phil Jackson and Horace Grant are even more impressive when we realize that Horace has an identical twin, Harvey, who was also a great basketball player in college. In fact, they were the tenth and twelfth players chosen in the NBA draft when they left college.

Harvey had an excellent, eleven-year career in the pros. Although his teams were never champions, his salaries totaled almost $23 million, in other words, just over $2 million a year for his career.

Horace, in contrast, played for sixteen years. The big differences? Horace was clearly lucky to be on better teams that won four championships—although he did have something to do with that, too. Some of the most noteworthy elements in a comparison of the twins' careers is that Horace's average rebounds per game were almost twice as good as Harvey's and he blocked twice as many shots per game, too. Thus, Horace devoted himself to doing the dirty work. I can't imagine that he liked doing it, but his teams always needed it and Phil Jackson constantly encouraged him to do it. His dedication also provided other benefits: he earned almost three times as much as his brother did during his career, with salaries totaling almost $68 million.

The moral of this story is clear: Phil Jackson was a remarkably successful coach. He seemed to dedicate himself and his team to a single, central goal, to win a championship. One important reason for his success was his ability to persuade his players to fill their roles and to persuade Horace Grant to do the dirty work that every team needs to do to achieve their ultimate goal. Any time Horace wanted to take more shots or be more involved in the team's offense, Jackson could repeat that (1) he needed Horace to do the dirty work and (2) it was really effective. Not only did Jackson succeed at his goals, but his strategy had significant positive effects for Horace as well.

Achieving Your Goals

When we look beyond organizational goals, we encounter personal goals. Have you fulfilled all of your goals in life? Most people haven't. Instead, we tend to find ourselves some distance away from where we would ultimately like to be, professionally and personally. Most people are motivated to achieve their goals, and the more important the goal, the stronger their motivation tends to be.

As we pursue our goals, we typically think about what we need to do next. This is perfectly natural. The problem with this approach, however, is that the farther we are from a goal, the less we know about what our next step should be. If, for example, I wanted the business schools of the world to change what they teach and how they teach it so that future leaders could avoid disastrous events like the recent financial meltdown, it would be particularly difficult for me to identify what I should do first, even though I have a variety of exciting ideas about how to achieve this goal.

Let's depict this general situation in the following way. Let's start with two states of nature: your current state (your starting point) and a possible future state (your ultimate goal). For the sake of our analysis, let's also assume that you are currently some distance, in time and space, from your ultimate goal:

**You Are
Here**

◎

**Your Ultimate
Goal Is Here**

GOAL

Obviously, we need to move toward our goal to ultimately achieve it. Thus, our natural inclination is to think about what we will do next—what will our next step be?

Although this is natural, it turns out that a logical extension of chapter 2's Leadership Law suggests a better plan. Just as leaders should think about the reactions they would like to achieve and mold their actions to achieve it, we should think first about our desired end state—the achievement of our goal—and what we need to do to achieve it. Because we may not be perfectly clear about what our next step should be, we should focus instead on what our *last step* needs to be and see what we can do to get there, one step away from our ultimate goal. (This is the same idea as reverse engineering, transferred to the realm of individual behavior.)

This completely reverses the strategic process. But think what it accomplishes. First, we are more certain about the effectiveness of our last step than we are about the effectiveness of our next step: because it is so close to our ultimate goal, it is often easy to see what that last step needs to be. Thus, we now have much more clarity that we are on the right track. Second, if we can get to a point where we actually are one step away from our goal, its realization becomes infinitely more likely:

Then, to continue this process logically, we should move backwards, step by step, from that last step to the next-to-last step, to the step before that, and so on, and finally to our first step. By starting at the end and moving backwards to where we are now, we can get a far clearer idea of how to approach our ultimate goals most efficiently, right from the start.

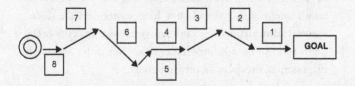

This process, derived from the formal economics of game theory, is called *backwards induction*: start at the end, at where you want to be, and work your way back to the beginning, choosing your first step so that it logically sets up the next, which will logically set up the next, and the next after that.

Backwards Induction

This technique is tremendously useful for all sorts of leadership decisions. To see how it works for a person's ultimate career goals, let's work through a real-life example.

After working in universities for more than forty years, I have met many, many professors. A few of them have confided to me that they would someday like to be a university president. I'm always shocked at these revelations, because this is something I have never, ever wanted to be. In fact, I've done my best to avoid as many administrative jobs as I can. So when a friend tells me she would like to be a university president someday, I have to get over the shock of the idea before I can think about whether and how this kind of achievement might be possible.

It clearly is possible, at least for some of my faculty colleagues. If they start at the end and work backwards, here is how this process could go:

1. The last step before becoming a university president is to be a senior university administrator. Universities almost never hire their presidents from among the set of general faculty members; instead they hire someone with documented administrative experience because university presidents tend to be administrators first: they don't act much like normal, everyday faculty members.

2. To get a senior administrative position, a faculty member must have been involved in fund-raising, because this is one of a university president's most important tasks. It is also often a prerequisite for a senior administrative position. Thus, the next-to-last step in this process is to establish a record of successful fund-raising.

3. To be able to raise money, a person must have had a junior administrative position: once again, universities don't want everyday faculty members to take the initiative, on their own, to raise money. If they did, things could get pretty chaotic, and university development offices run best when they coordinate their activities well.

4. To get to backwards step number 3, above, a faculty member almost always needs to be a tenured full professor. To get to this position, they must have had a successful research career. It also helps to be a good teacher. This creates three more backwards steps in the process (tenure, research record, and teaching record).

5. To become a faculty member, most universities require a PhD, preferably from a top school. (However much we might want to argue that universities are not elitist, they are: graduation from a top school opens many more doors than graduation from a middle-of-the-road school does.) To get into a top PhD program, a student needs very good grades, excellent test scores, and outstanding letters of recommendation, preferably from a top undergraduate school.

6. To get into a top undergraduate school, a high school student must also get good grades, excellent test scores, and outstanding letters of recommendation.

Thus, to ultimately become a university president, you must start your strategic planning at about age fifteen.

Ha! Obviously, this is not the only path to becoming a university president. But it does highlight a particularly efficient path; it also identifies the sine qua non of achieving this goal—the steps that are absolutely necessary, "without which you have nothing." It would be incredibly rare, for instance, for a university to hire someone without a PhD as their president. In fact, if my colleague wanted to be a university president at a top school and she had received her PhD from a mediocre school, her chances would also be extremely slim. If she had a poor research record, she would have almost no chance at all because other faculty members wouldn't respect her and would therefore be unlikely supporters.

Many of the steps in this process are not just important but essential; taking them in order also makes the process easier, clearer, and more direct. In many ways, it lets you do less. This is why backwards induction is so useful: it's a tremendously rational approach to achieving your career goals, and it highlights how missteps can lengthen your career path unnecessarily, or even disqualify you forever. It also emphasizes the natural path of great leaders' careers: early on, you must accumulate skills; in the middle (which can be very brief), you must use those skills and show your mettle; and later, as you move up, you must do less and less. Ultimately, your goal should be to *Do Nothing!* even as you are simultaneously becoming increasingly effective.

Another Example

What if your goal was to become the president of the United States? Bill Clinton did, and he announced this goal when he was thirteen. A short thirty-three years later, at the age of forty-six, he became the nation's third youngest president. Did he use backwards induction to get there? Thankfully, it's hard for any of us to accurately remember all of our thought patterns when we were teenagers. Thus, whether or when Clinton might have used backwards induction is impossible to determine. At the same time, the pattern of his life and its ultimate success (even before it is over) looks very much as if he planned almost every step along the way. Here's why:

In high school, Clinton was an active student leader, and now reminisces about his early hopes of pursuing elective office: "I loved music and thought I could be very good, but I knew I would never be John Coltrane or Stan Getz. I was interested in medicine and thought I could be a fine doctor, but I knew I would never be Michael DeBakey. But I knew I could be great in public service." Although college might have been tough on his family financially, he won a scholarship to go to Georgetown, which gave him the opportunity to learn about foreign policy right at the epicenter of U.S. politics. During his undergraduate years, he also interned for Arkansas senator J. William Fulbright, getting a firsthand glimpse of a successful politician in action. After Georgetown, he won a

Rhodes Scholarship—a tremendous coup for both his education and his résumé—and then he returned to the States to attend Yale Law School. In law school, he worked in the 1972 McGovern campaign and led McGovern's effort in Texas. After graduation he became a law professor at the University of Arkansas; the next year he ran for the House of Representatives and lost. In 1976, he was elected Arkansas attorney general (without opposition). At the grand old age of thirty-two, he was elected governor of Arkansas, the youngest governor in the country. He lost his next election but was reelected two years after that and remained governor for ten years. It's fairly obvious that those two electoral losses were not part of his plan. But his lengthy tenure as Arkansas's governor gave him time to build a broad base of support that he needed to achieve his goal of becoming president.

In 1992, Clinton won the presidential election against Republican incumbent George H. W. Bush and billionaire populist Ross Perot. As noted, there is almost no way to get accurate retrospective evidence to verify that he used backwards induction as he proceeded toward the presidency; but his actions, his recollections, and his career trajectory suggest that he may have actually engaged in a similar process.

In addition, after leaving office, like many ex-presidents, it seems as if he has created new goals for himself that might not have been obtainable otherwise. It is possible that, along the way, he revised and updated his ultimate goals—which is perfectly appropriate as you achieve each new goal. So even the presidency might have been just one step along a path to his (new) ultimate goals.

Conclusions

The general principles of backwards induction apply in many contexts, particularly for leaders, as the Leadership Law is a particularly important example of backwards induction. In engineering and in software development, when a company wants to discover how a product was made, it helps to take it apart—to work from a completed model to identify its elemental parts and how they are put together, in other words, reverse engineering.

In the context of personal goals, backwards induction focuses on the end point and the next-to-last step rather than on your next action, when you may not know all of the strategic contingencies. By working backwards, it is far easier to identify all of the necessary steps and their prerequisites, in the necessary order, to achieve what you want.

Another of the leadership implications of backwards induction is that most successful plans require a series of incremental steps. It is extremely difficult, and rare, for leaders and their teams to make quantum leaps from their current achievement level to their desired, hoped-for goals. In addition, effective leaders realize that they can't achieve their leadership goals in a single step (backwards induction). As a leader you must influence your team members to help you move gradually, rationally, and incrementally, because achieving your ultimate goals almost always requires a deliberate, multistep process.

By logically working backwards to the present, you can identify all of the critical interim goals and benchmarks you will need to meet before you ultimately reach your desired end state. Put simply, to build a mansion, you must build a foundation that can support its roof. If you will be installing a heavy, slate roof, it will need to be a particularly strong foundation. If you build a weaker foundation, you can't have a slate roof—ever. Taking the appropriate early steps preserves your opportunities to achieve great things later. To achieve your ultimate career goals, you will need to build teams that will allow you to do less. By not micromanaging, you can get the kind of assistance you need to be successful as a leader and, simultaneously, achieve your goals. You can't do it all by yourself and, paradoxically, by Doing Nothing, you can help your team members feel that they are not being micromanaged, and they can more readily fulfill their own potentials. Plotting this process via backwards induction markedly increases your chances of success.

Like the Leadership Law, each step of the backwards induction process is at least somewhat uncertain—but by starting at the end, rather than at the beginning, and working backwards, you also create opportunities to revise your strategies whenever you fall off your ideal path.

4

Trust More

MY BROTHER KEVIN arrived 472 days after I was born. Until I got married, we shared the same room. We both worked part-time jobs when we were in high school and we both liked clothes, so much so that they consumed most of our meager earnings. We also had an added advantage: for at least a couple years, our sizes were pretty much the same. This meant that our fairly separate groups of friends thought that each of us had an amazing wardrobe, even though we wore the same set of clothes (and even shared the same closet). The big downside, however, was that we went to an all-boys high school, so our fancy duds didn't get us very far with girls.

It's been a long time since high school, and my tastes in clothes have changed (thankfully). After far too many missteps along the way, I now realize that I particularly like Italian designers. This means that I try to wear Italian suits and jackets when I teach—brands like Giorgio Armani, Ermenegildo Zegna, Versace, and Canali. (I also mix in Hugo Boss, Ralph Lauren, Burberry, and

Brooks Brothers, but they don't have as much cachet as the Italian guys do.)

As you probably know, Italian clothes can be pretty expensive. On a recent Web site listing, for instance, the retail prices of several Canali suits ranged from $1,500 to $1,695, and a Valentino tuxedo (silk) was $3,190. Sale prices may be less, but these are still pretty expensive clothes.

When I wear Italian to class, I make sure that my students (mostly executives and executive MBAs) see the designer's name on the label of my jackets—not to show off, but to get their attention so that I can share some informal research data. You see, I have paid more than $100 for a jacket or a suit only once, and there is a lovely Hugo Boss suit in my closet that cost a grand total of $28.

So when my executive students discover the names on the labels of my jackets, I also make sure they learn how much I paid for them. Again, not to show off, even though it does get their attention. They typically ask me whether I have been to a local rummage sale or if I am related to a thief! The actual source is eBay.

Buying from eBay

At the time of this writing, my reputation on eBay is 1265, which means that I have had 1,265 different interactions on eBay, mostly purchases of books, DVDs, and CDs, but also clothes, furniture, jewelry, toys, and gifts. Of these 1,265 interactions, I have only had 8 bad experiences, and I have lost money on only 4 (see Figure 1). I do my homework: I buy from reputable sellers and I try to avoid what seems like stolen merchandise (for example, many identical items for sale by the same seller). But even then, the ratio of my good experiences to my bad experiences is still pretty impressive, isn't it? That ratio is 1,257 to 8, and it includes many, many good deals, and a host of wonderful stories of conscientious, trustworthy sellers and buyers.

At the same time, I can tell you *minute details* about each of the 8 bad experiences. They sometimes included a series of angry, argumentative e-mail exchanges; they were always a hassle and some of them led to lost sleep. But a simple, rational evaluation—1,257 positive interactions to only 8 bad ones, and a closet full of clothes that no university faculty member should be able to afford—makes it obvious that the positives far outweigh the negatives.

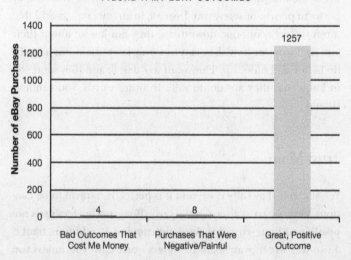

FIGURE 1. MY EBAY OUTCOMES

When I buy jackets or suits on eBay, I deal with sellers whom I will never meet: they are complete and utter strangers. I know their selling history and their reputation from other buyers, but they have no face, no name, only an eBay ID. I send them money (the value of the final, successful bid plus shipping charges) and they send me what I won.

They can take my money and change their identity on eBay and start selling again tomorrow, and I would have almost no recourse.* Yet nearly all of them are completely trustworthy, and many are more than trustworthy: many times sellers have let me know that there's a problem with an auction item *before* they send it to me. I've had eBay sellers identify problems that I would never have noticed. In every case, they apologize for the problem and then they do everything they can to make it right.

The bottom line is this: if I can trust anonymous strangers on eBay, how much should you trust the people you work with? They are not strangers; they want to keep their jobs; they do *not* wake up in the morning thinking of ways they can make mistakes, or perform poorly, or screw you. Instead, in an uncertain world that often suffers economic downturns, they think a lot about their jobs and wonder how they can not only keep them but actually do better and move up. They want to do well; and they want you to know that they are doing well. In other words, you can and should . . .

Trust More

Yes, it can feel awfully risky, and it is perfectly natural to be cautious, because trust always entails risk. But great leadership is not possible without trust: it is absolutely *required*. In addition, trust is a two-way street: your team members won't trust you unless you trust them—and more trust is certainly better than less.

---

* eBay's partner firm, PayPal, has an appeal process that can get buyers the purchase price back, but it's quite a hassle and a lengthy process, and it has monetary limits.

The Intuition

Have you ever seen a supervisor, a boss, or an authority figure trust someone more than they anticipated? This can happen in a team meeting or a one-on-one interaction when a boss gives someone a more challenging job, with more discretion and authority than they ever expect.

For the last seven years, I have asked the executives in my classes if they have ever had this experience; about half of them raise their hands. When I ask them how they have responded to this experience, *they all have exactly the same answer:* they say that, when they were trusted more than they expected, they stepped up and exerted extra effort to show the person who had trusted them that they were worthy of their trust. Every single one.

This makes for a very clear message. If you want to be a more effective leader, if you want to get the same response that all of my executives' bosses got, simply do what they did. Trust More. The result will be positive reciprocity, which will make your job easier and allow you to move much closer to actually Doing Nothing.

Trust, Risk, and Fear

Why don't leaders trust people more? In a word, *fear:* leaders (and other people) are afraid that if they trust someone too much, their trust will boomerang on them, and they will be hurt more than if they hadn't trusted at all. People are naturally cautious: it takes them awhile to be comfortable enough to trust people more.

This fearful rationale is correct in one respect: trusting always entails risk. Whom to trust, when, and how much should depend on what you know about the person and the situation. You must do your homework. You should never trust blindly. New employees should always have probationary periods to prove themselves, and no boss should ever hire a convicted felon to handle a cash business.

A little conscientious homework, however, is all that is needed to make trusting action effective. Before bidding on eBay, for instance, I always look at a seller's reputation: how many buyers have commented on this seller's previous performance, and how positive have they been? I try to avoid bidding on merchandise that is being sold by anyone whose reputation is less than 98 percent and by anyone who has sold fewer than one hundred items.

This also plays out at work. Bill was a high-tech manager who was coordinating a big, six-month project that was larger and longer than his normal projects. As a result, he was encouraged to recruit help from other project teams to stay ahead of his deadlines. Jim was recommended by another team leader and seemed to have some of the skills that Bill needed, so Bill invited him onboard and gave him a task that fit his advertised competencies.

Whenever Bill checked on Jim's progress, Jim assured him that things were going well and that he was right on track. Bill had a lot to accomplish, so he left Jim to his work and checked again, intermittently.

As it turned out, Jim did not have the requisite skills, his part of the project was way behind schedule, and Bill found himself in a major bind. The root of the problem? Being too anxious to get going on the project and not doing his homework. Jim and his previous manager overpromised—and this would have been obvious if Bill had paid more attention to Jim's previous jobs and his performance on them. Had he done his homework, he still might have recruited Jim, but he also could have gotten Jim the training he needed to do the job. As it was, the project didn't finish until far beyond its deadline and Bill paid dearly for being late.

Doing your homework is critical in any situation involving trust. People are often tempted to promise more than they can deliver, and when they do, those of us who have trusted them pay the price. The only way to avoid these costs is to know as much as you can about the people you are dealing with and, when you trust, realize that there is *always* a chance that your trust will be violated, inadvertently or on purpose.

It never feels good to trust someone and then be exploited. When someone violates your trust, the consequences can be sizable, both substantively and emotionally, and the negative impact tends to be much greater than the positive effects that result when people honor your trust. When things go well, it's great, but when things go badly, it can feel really, really bad.

In addition, a bad trusting experience can lead to disproportionate increases in our fears that it will happen again. Bill, for example, became far more gun-shy after the Jim fiasco. Because fear is such a strong emotion, it makes negative outcomes from trusting particularly memorable, and this can have a huge impact on our future action choices. Think, for instance, of times when someone's romance has gone bad. It often sours them on *any* romance, for quite some time. As the saying goes, "once bitten, twice shy." These kinds of memories lead people to have fear when they trust, and because emotions dominate reason, people often choose not to trust when they might have benefited tremendously.

In fact, the research on this is very clear: bad outcomes tend to seriously outweigh comparable good outcomes because they are *vivid, available* events. Our memories are not egalitarian: we remember events that stand out, and negatives stand out much more than positives do. This is particularly true for people who have trusted and been burned: trust violations are vivid, emotionally charged events. As a result, they affect us deeply and they influence our subsequent decision making much more than positive outcomes do.

It seems clear that, even though leaders remember the pain they suffered from untrustworthy behavior, they tend to trust too little and, as a result, they miss out on many of the benefits they could derive from mutual trust. Add to this the fact that many leaders deal with people who are professionals—that is, people who care about their jobs—and it's clear that leaders fail to take advantage of their many trusting opportunities.

Here again, it pays for leaders to think about the Leadership Law and the reactions that their actions will provoke. Professionals work in all sorts of jobs, from low-level managerial positions to handling shipments at the company's loading dock. In the simplest and most important sense, professionals are people who want to do their jobs well. The basic notion of being a professional leads to all sorts of positive consequences at work. In particular, it suggests that professionals are smart enough to know that it pays to be trustworthy; they may also want to be trustworthy for its own sake (to maintain their own positive self-identities).

There's even more involved here. People around the world, in every culture, have a universal, natural reaction *to reciprocate*. Doing a favor for someone or giving them a gift typically leads people to respond in kind: you scratch my back, I'll scratch yours. Turn taking is normal and natural, in almost every society. It is also another reason why executives consistently step up when they've been trusted more than they expect: they reciprocate their leaders' trust in them.

By trusting more, leaders can start a positive chain of reciprocity. Taking a risk with a professional has a very high probability of resulting in the person's stepping up and doing their best. This allows leaders to trust them more, and a continuing positive cycle can result. In contrast, when leaders don't trust much, they and their team members not only miss a golden opportunity to create the mutual benefits that come from trusting actions, they may also be starting a *negative* chain of reciprocity because, in the absence of trust, people tend to be suspicious, and when an opportunity for trust is not taken, suspiciousness and all of the negatives that accompany it can grow. Thus, the fulcrum between trusting and not trusting can be extremely narrow but it is truly critical: falling on one side or the other can lead to great positives or serious negatives—as a result of either a small act of trust or its absence.

Most leaders also interact with the same groups of people over and over again: they tend to work with the same team members; their best customers tend to come back repeatedly; and stable relationships with suppliers are so mutually beneficial that both buyers and sellers reap great benefit from long-term, mutually reinforcing interactions. In short, many of our interactions are with people we know. These kinds of relationships drastically reduce the likelihood that people will violate our trust. In other words, most of the people we interact with are likely to be much more trustworthy than strangers on eBay—and 99.37 percent of my eBay encounters have been with people who were completely trustworthy. This makes it clear that, at work, the risks of trusting are nowhere near as high as they are on eBay—or in other areas of life. For you as a leader, it pays to trust your team members more because it leads to tremendously positive reactions, building positively reciprocal relationships, and it pays for you, too, as it makes it much easier for you to *Do Nothing!*

At the same time, because it is natural to have fear when it comes to trust, keep thinking about my Italian clothes as you try to overcome your fears. Do your best to Trust More—maybe not a lot more at first, but at least a little more: ask yourself if you can trust any of the people on your team more than you do now. Most people can, and when they act on that realization, their team members tend to appreciate it immensely and respond in kind. One final tip: when you trust people more, let them know what you are doing. In particular, tell them that you're sorry that you haven't trusted them more before and that it was your fault, not theirs. Adding an apology to a trust boost almost inevitably leads to powerful positive reactions.

A Proverb and a Model

An old Japanese proverb, "Every stranger is a thief," doesn't convey much confidence in the trustworthiness of our fellow human beings. It's about as pessimistic as you can get. At the same time, it avoids risks and it reflects what researchers call "a rational approach to trust development" (see Figure 2). This approach suggests that you should not trust people you don't know until you have had repeated positive interactions with them. Then your trust can increase.

This rational model also suggests that there is a limit to trust, as the S-curve flattens out at the top. For instance, you might never loan anyone an extremely large sum of money.

Leaders who live by this model express it directly when they say to their team members, "You must earn my trust." When a team member performs well repeatedly, these leaders tend to relax and trust them more—but it can feel like a grudgingly slow process to the individuals who are earning their trust. These leaders do not qualify as Trust More leaders; they are Trust Very Slowly leaders and, as a result, they miss many golden opportunities.

This is just one approach. At the other extreme are the rare leaders who give people their trust right from the start. One example is an executive whom I will call Alice, who trusted people completely, in a particularly unusual way. She worked for a small company that had three locations, X, Y, and Z, each about two hundred miles away from the other. She was an up-and-coming young manager, relatively early in her career, when word spread throughout the company about a huge mistake that someone had made at location X. Alice worked at location Y, but when she heard about the mistake, she piped up and said, "That was all my fault. I'll take the blame. I apologize."

Frankly, people looked at her like she was crazy: she could not have made the mistake—she was two hundred miles away. But no one said anything; they just scratched their heads at Alice's strange admission and then they all got back to work.

The next time someone made a big mistake, Alice stepped up and apologized again. In fact, ever since that first event, she has taken the blame for every big mistake anyone makes in any of the company's three locations.

Foolhardy? Suicidal? Just plain crazy? Actually, Alice has now established a reputation for herself as "The Big Apologizer." Whenever she apologizes—and she apologizes for anyone and everyone's mistakes—everyone shakes their heads, laughs, and then—most important—they move on. By apologizing, Alice has

FIGURE 2. A RATIONAL MODEL OF TRUST DEVELOPMENT

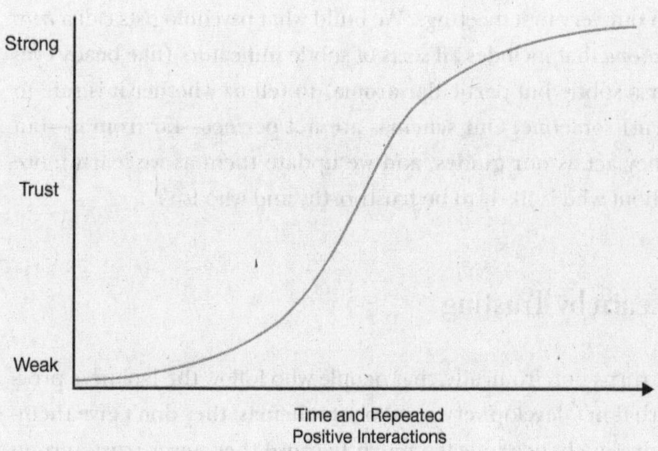

Strong

Trust

Weak

Time and Repeated
Positive Interactions

helped her company turn the corner and look forward each time someone makes a mistake, rather than looking back and getting caught up in the "blame game." Not only that, Alice reports that this has not hurt her career at all; instead, she has been promoted faster than she ever anticipated.

The key element here is that Alice trusted her colleagues. She put herself into a tremendously vulnerable position because she trusted that her colleagues knew her well enough to realize she was apologizing for a good reason rather than out of lunacy. Not only was she rewarded, but now her colleagues are less fearful that they will get in huge trouble if they make a mistake. They can concentrate on doing their best possible work and know that, if things go wrong, Alice has their back. Her actions have also helped her company be more forward-looking and progressive, rather than backwards-looking and regressive. It's all based on trust that didn't cost Alice a thing. Instead, she benefited from it, too.

Most of us fall between these two extremes: we trust more than the Japanese proverb recommends but we don't trust our colleagues as much as Alice trusted hers. In fact, as we go through life, we learn to trust some people and not to trust others, even in our very first meetings. We build what psychologists call a *trust schema* that includes all sorts of subtle indicators (like beady eyes or a subtle but particular aroma) to tell us whether it is safe to trust someone. Our schemas are not perfect—far from it—but they act as our guides, and we update them as we learn more about who is likely to be trustworthy and who isn't.

Learn by Trusting

It turns out, ironically, that people who follow the Japanese proverb don't develop very good trust schemas: they don't give themselves a chance to learn much because they never trust anyone they don't know. Professors Nancy Carter of the University of Toronto and Mark Weber of the University of Waterloo have recently found that people who have a strong proclivity to trust learn more from their experience and develop better skills at detecting lies; in contrast, people who have an aversion to trusting never find out who might actually have been trustworthy. Their research gives us another reason to trust people more: by trusting, we learn more and we make better trusting decisions in the future. Does this mean we should entrust our life savings to a stranger? Obviously not. But a calculated gamble now and then can truly pay off, in outcomes and in learning.

Here's one of many possible examples. I recently presented a two-day negotiation workshop for a company in Shanghai. I arrived on Thursday, had a good night's sleep, presented a series of negotiation exercises and lessons on Friday and Saturday, and had most of Sunday free before my flight home. I asked my host where I could shop for unique, local gifts and he directed me to the Old City of Shanghai. (When I arrived, I realized that my wife, who knows China well, had taken us to the same area several years before.) The place was bustling with locals and only a few tourists. I wandered around and discovered quite a few unique gifts for my family.

All morning long I was approached by young Chinese men trying to sell me watches or flowers or, seemingly, anything they had at hand. Responses of "No, thank you" always led them to persist—relentlessly. Needless to say, this got old very quickly. Finally I discovered a solution—I stopped responding. This went against everything I was taught as a child—to be polite to everyone. But it worked very well.

After puttering around for several hours, I was getting really hungry. I walked into two restaurants but both were immensely crowded and it appeared that people were getting their food in several different locations and then paying for it in several other

locations and it seemed like an incredibly confusing arrange-
ment for someone who doesn't speak Chinese. What I really
wanted was a restaurant where I could sit down and order from a
menu, hopefully one with pictures or some English text. By now,
however, my stomach was speaking to me, loudly.

As I kept looking for a place to eat, another Chinese man
started to talk to me. As before, I didn't say anything, at which
point he said, "So, you are going to ignore me?" I turned and saw
a gentleman, about sixty years old, wearing a Yankees baseball
cap. He said, "I'm not trying to sell you anything." I apologized,
explaining about my experiences that morning and my solution, to not say anything. He then said, "What are you looking
for?" When I told him I was hungry, he asked me, "Do you like
tea?" I'm not sure how he knew to ask this question, as I love tea
and drink many cups a day.

When I responded positively (still being cautious), he told me
about two tea shops in the area that also served light lunches—he
referred to the food as snacks, with a long "n": *snnnnacks*. Movie
stars, he said, had recently visited one place so they had raised
their prices. The other place was a school where people learned
about tea. He said that it was reasonable and that they allowed
customers to try as many different kinds of tea as they wanted. I
expressed interest, and he said he would be happy to take me
there.

It was at this point that I took a risk: I asked him to be my guest
for lunch.

My oh-so-rational reasoning? He was pleasant company and I
didn't think I would lose too much money having tea and some
snacks. They could certainly overcharge me, but how much? I
thought that the downside risk was pretty small, and the upside
was that this could become an adventure.

As it turned out, the snacks were simple, tasty dumplings and the tea was delicious. I tried ten different varieties. The bill for the two of us was a grand total of $15. We also had a very pleasant conversation and he hailed me a cab after lunch so I could get to the airport in plenty of time.

All in all, it was a lovely experience. Who would think, in a city of over ten million people, halfway around the world, that a stranger would be so helpful, so friendly, and so kind? A small risk led to a lovely day that showed how trustworthy people can be. If this can happen in Shanghai, with a complete stranger, what is likely to happen with people you work with, with people in your own neighborhood or your own town? The odds of a trustworthy response make small risks easily worth taking, and even some large risks, too.

My eBay data, as well as my experience in Shanghai, as informal as they are, suggest that people tend to be pretty darn trustworthy. This makes particular sense at work, because people at work understand how important their reputations are and this pushes them to do whatever they can to retain, preserve, and grow a positive reputation. This is a truly time-consuming process.

People try to do well and to put themselves in position to be evaluated positively; both strategies make them highly likely to be trustworthy. The sad part is that most leaders don't realize this, or at least they act as if they don't. In particular, trust at work is a perfect context for understanding how important the Leadership Law is: by trusting more, with people who are more trustworthy than we realize, we stimulate reactions that are so good that everyone benefits. Your team members will not only feel more trusted, they will usually do more and you can do less, to the point of Doing Nothing. This reiterates the conclusion that most leaders trust too little and, as a result, do too much. Trusting More will help you Do Nothing; trust less and you can't.

Your Glorious Career

Let's take this further and consider your next promotion. Let's assume you have done well and have moved up the corporate ladder at a fairly brisk pace and that your next promotion is substantial. Our scenario goes something like this:

Your supervisor comes to your office and announces, "Congratulations. It's time for your next promotion, a big one!" Needless to say, this is good news. In fact, it turns out to be more than good news as your promotion is bigger than you expected—you have just been given the position you have always wanted. You will now be leading a group that is already successful, in a challenging, growing area of the firm. It's a dream come true.

You have heard great things about your new team: they are all professionals and each of them has been working for the firm for a year or more. They are all competent, and informal scuttlebutt indicates that they perform well as a team. At the same time, you are confident that you can bring some new ideas and some new energy so that the team can achieve even more. You are charged up and ready to go.

There is a bit of time before your formal appointment begins. Although this is a dream-come-true job, you naturally have some questions. Most of all, you want to learn about your new team members. In particular, you would like to know:

1. How competent they are.
2. How trustworthy they are.
3. Whether they have any personality conflicts that interfere with their performance.

You would like to learn even more about your team members, but you focus on these three, essential pieces of information. The boss has scheduled a meeting to introduce you to the team and, before that meeting, you would like to know how things stand. Therefore, you seek out the team's current, soon-to-be leaving leader who is about to retire. She is amazingly open and helpful and tells you everything that she possibly can about each of the team members.

Your second step is to look at the new team members' personnel files. Not surprisingly, they are only mildly informative: they reveal when each person was hired, their initial and current positions, their latest evaluations (the most helpful information in the file), a good description of their current job responsibilities, and a few pieces of demographic data. The files are fairly disappointing, though, because they don't have the kinds of specific information that would tell you as much as you want to know about your three critical issues.

You realize that, although your two sources of information have been helpful, they are both limited. In particular, as helpful as their current leader has been, she can only tell you about the team members' previous interactions—she can't say how they will interact with you. You have also talked with other people who have worked with the team, but they don't have the kinds of fine-grained information that you are looking for either. You have a picture of each of the new team members, but it is obviously far from complete. At the same time, you are still really excited about this great new opportunity.

If you are proud of being rational, and you are seriously concerned about not making a misstep as the team's new leader, you might naturally follow the rational model of trust development (Figure 2) and do what many new leaders do: give each team member a small task.* In your mind, these are actually

---

* Many newly appointed leaders also choose to have one-on-one meetings with their new team members, to introduce themselves and to get a "feel" for each of them. For leaders who are truly adept interpersonally, this can work very well. Even then, however, there is the serious danger of inadvertently pressing someone's "hot

tests, but you don't reveal this to your team members. You are hoping that their performances will reveal their competencies and the range of their skills, and a small task means you are not risking much.

As it happens, all of your new team members come back with thoroughly mediocre performance—at best. They have not done well at all, and your wonderful dream-come-true job now seems like a nightmare.

Not so fast. In fact, you have learned *absolutely nothing*.

Why? First, all of the new team members are professionals and have been with the company for more than a year. In other words, they know what they are doing and what they are capable of.

More important, their antennae are out, big-time. They've heard that they are getting a new leader and they are understandably curious about what you will be like and, even more, how you will treat them. Also, because they have been working together as a team for some time, it's natural for them to talk about you and wonder what you will be like. It's also natural for them to compare notes about the first job you've given them. It wouldn't take much for them to realize that you are testing them and that you are not showing them much respect. In fact, as professionals, they are likely to be offended at the piddly little jobs you have given them.

In essence, your natural tendencies—and a rational model—have led you to fail your first test as their new leader, and you have not failed in a small way: you have failed *miserably*. They think of their first, small task as a signal of how much you trust them (not much); you have gotten absolutely no useful information about their competence and their trustworthiness; and worst of all, you have insulted them.

---

buttons"—touching on particularly sensitive issues, insensitively—and really getting off on the wrong foot, *fast*.

Thus, even though you were trying to be careful, even though you didn't want to take a big risk, even though you thought you were being completely rational, your first leadership act in your great new job, the job you have always dreamed of, is a step in exactly the wrong direction. You have just stuck your foot in it, as we say here in Illinois, and first impressions are tremendously powerful. None of this is good, for you or for your new team.

In fact, many new leaders who get a job they have always wanted soon discover that their new job is not what they thought it would be, that their new team is not as competent and motivated as they had hoped, and that their work is really cut out for them. How can you get out of this all-too-enticing trap?

Earlier in this chapter, we discussed what happens when a boss or supervisor trusts someone more than they anticipated. Executives' consistently unanimous responses provide a critical clue to how this situation could have gone much better.

You started out well by doing your homework: you tried to find out as much as you could about the team and its members. But you didn't get an A in preparation. Here's the critical and surprising part that you missed (naturally): although you checked out your team members' personnel files, you didn't use them as well as you could have. Even though they may seem like fairly sad repositories of insufficient information, they are actually a gold mine of important data because they can tell you what each of your team members has been working on as well as what they are qualified to do.

For instance, if one of your team members has skills and gets special assignments in spectography, his personnel file will include that information. If another of your team members has been the point person in initiating dialogue with potential new customers, her personnel file will reveal that information, too. If a third team member knows how to coordinate the work of several independent, snarly subcontractors, flawlessly, this is likely to be noted as well. In other words, you could boost your grade and get an A+ on your homework if you used your team members' personnel files to identify two key facts: what they have been currently working on and how competent they are. This information is invaluable, as it gives you a good idea of the kinds of tasks you can confidently assign to each of them. In particular, it gives you clues about *how you can trust your team members more than they think they will be trusted* in your very first job assignments.

This strategy means you are trusting people more, immediately. The hard part is to gauge the exact details of their first assignments—you don't want to trust them a great deal more than they have been trusted before because they may not be ready for that much trust. You also don't want to give them tasks that are outside their skill sets, as that would set them up for failure. But those seemingly inadequate personnel files can actually help you to identify a new, first job that entrusts them with *a bit more* than what they've been working on lately—a bit more challenge, a bit more responsibility, and a bit more discretion. Not a lot more, but a bit more. You can tell them you have heard great things about them; you can tell them you trust them to do well; and you can tell them you think they can accomplish even more than they have already been accomplishing.

What are their reactions likely to be?

By trusting competent professionals more than they anticipated, you send a strong signal—that you trust them, right from the start, and that they don't have to prove it. They don't have to "earn" your trust; they get it right away. They start out being trusted, at their very first meeting with their new leader. For people who enjoy their work and who are proud of what they can do (professionals) this is a strong, positive signal.

In fact, you can do the same thing with your current team members. They will appreciate it, too.

Our research suggests that trusting more is not just a good first signal. When a team of professionals is trusted more than they expected and each of them steps up to reciprocate and show their new leader that they are worthy of her trust, they put you and your new team on the fast track to mutual trust, on the black curve of Figure 3 rather than the normal but far slower gray curve. These kinds of teams gain enormous benefits, in both performance and outcomes, way beyond the results that "You must earn my trust" leaders can obtain.

It also means that your new team members are doing more than they ever have (and they are loving it, too). Where does this leave you? Doing Nothing! (Or far less than you might have imagined.)

Here's another way to think of this process. Have you ever seen a work team that really clicks? Right from the start? Whether this is the result of a chemical connection or some other

FIGURE 3. THE RESULTS (IN BLACK) OF TRUSTING MORE VS. "YOU MUST EARN MY TRUST" (IN GRAY)

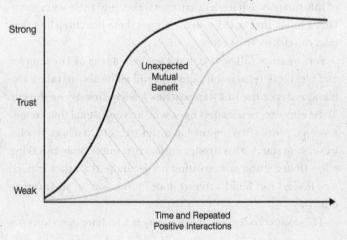

undetectable source, some groups mesh *immediately*. They work extraordinarily well together—and they trust one another right from the beginning.

That's not all. Think of your team members' reactions at the end of their first day, when they go home and see their friends and family. They are bound to talk about their brand new leader, and what do you think they will they say? "You wouldn't believe what happened to me today. We met our new team leader and she trusted me more than my previous leader, who worked with me for three years, ever did." Clearly, this is a good start for a new leader and her new team.

Will it work for everyone? Obviously not. Some people don't want new challenges and some people don't want more responsibility. But by trusting people more than they anticipated, new leaders not only can jump-start their teams; they can also learn an enormous amount, and do less. In addition, they can immediately learn how competent and how trustworthy their new team members are. This information is golden—knowing people's skills and knowing who is trustworthy are incredibly useful pieces of information that leaders can't get if they give their team members a small, first task. Leaders only get these benefits when they take the risk to Trust More.

Performance will be better, the team members will be happier and feel more responsible, and they will all be able to take a tremendously positive first step on a new leader's first day on the job. To be effective, new leaders must send a strong signal that creates a strong, *positive* first impression with their very first acts. It is far too easy to start with a strong, *negative* first impression. By taking a less-than-natural risk, trusting people more than they expect, new leaders can build a tremendous foundation for their future efforts.

These same concepts apply for leaders who have been working

with their team members for some time, because there is almost always room to Trust More. It may be harder to convince your long-standing team members that you have turned a corner, that you have a new outlook on life, and that you are ready to delegate responsibilities and challenges that you never delegated before. Tell them that you may be an old dog, but you have learned a new trick. If they don't believe you, mark up this page and show them this book. Then stand behind your decision and continue to Trust More. They will get the message, and they will look at you as if you are a new person (which you will be).

Why Don't We Do This More?

The decision to trust always entails risk, and research tells us that, naturally, trusters pay particular attention to their risks. The irony, however, is that the people they trust pay much less attention to their risks; instead, people who are trusted are naturally egocentric and pay more attention to the benefits they receive. This can cause a huge disconnect, with tremendous inefficiencies: potential trusters worry more than they should about their risks and don't realize that, if they trusted more, the people they trust would reciprocate more. In addition, when they hedge their "trust bets," the people they trust less also reciprocate less. In other words, a downward spiral of reciprocity may be far more likely than an upward, positive spiral.

When leaders face potentially trusting situations, their natural first question is To Trust or Not to Trust? Only after they answer this question affirmatively do they then consider *how much* they can afford to trust. In essence, their answer to this second question—How much to trust?—is often driven by the fears that result from having been burned in the past. As noted, leaders often get gun-shy when it comes to trust: they focus too much on their own risks and not enough on their team members' likely reactions.

This is the wrong way to approach trust. The big, critical first question will always be whether to trust, but the answer to this question should also answer your fears. Thus, if your answer to this question is "Yes," fear should no longer be part of the equation. Instead, the "How much?" question should not revolve around how much you should trust but around how much you can both gain by trusting. In other words, a leader who has decided to trust someone should be thinking about how much *more* they can trust them rather than how much they are risking: they have already turned the corner and committed to trust; now their view should be upward rather than downward, even though thinking about their risks is natural. This is another situation where you will do much better by avoiding your natural tendencies and realizing that once you're in, you're in—and now you should only be thinking about how far in you can go.

When the owners of sports teams hire a manager or a head coach, they look for someone who knows the game, who knows players, and who knows how to mix strategy with motivation. In almost every case, owners know less about managing than their managers do. Problems surface, however, when owners—who have more money as well as hiring and firing power—start to meddle with their teams. George Steinbrenner was notorious for doing this with the New York Yankees; Jerry Jones has a similar reputation with the Dallas Cowboys. It is easy to see that their meddling results from their being worried about their risks; they would do far better to choose their actions on the basis of the maximum benefit they might produce. If they did, they would meddle far less often, be less disruptive, and give their teams a better chance to win.

Here's another way to think about this, and something we can all relate to: how does it feel to be trusted partially (rather than completely)?

We all know the answer. Stated succinctly, *partial trust sucks*. When we know we have been trusted only partially, we naturally wonder, "Why didn't he trust me more?" This natural question reduces our motivation to reciprocate and leads to less long-term commitment to a leader, to a team, and to an organization. Partial trust sucks in many ways: it is the reverse of flattery and respect and it stimulates lousy outcomes, for everyone.

Rather than temporizing and hedging their bets and trusting partially, leaders do far better by trusting people more. Leaders take business risks all the time. Many leaders actually define themselves by the risks they take. As one executive put it, "If you are not willing to assume risks, go deal with another business." Another felt that "Risk taking is synonymous with decision making."

Leaders can naturally and easily think about their financial risks by weighing the upsides and the downsides. It's far less natural for them to think that their interactions with people have similar upsides and downsides. Instead, we tend to naturally think about the possible downsides of our interactions at work, because "bads" consistently outweigh "goods" in our memories.

The solution is to continue to follow the logic of the Leadership Law and to think of others' reactions before choosing our own actions. By realizing how well people respond to trust, you can get past your irrational fears and trust your team members, your suppliers, and your customers more.

You can also diversify your interpersonal risks as a leader the same way you diversify your investment risks. Trusting many people more spreads your leadership risks. You will do very well if you think of trusting your team members in the same way that you think of your stock portfolio, especially if you have a strong personal attachment to your financial investments. (I hope you have strong personal attachments to your team members, too.) Put simply: love your money and diversify; love your team members and diversify. This same simple strategy—one that people follow less than they should in both realms—can help you reap more monetary *and* more interpersonal gains.

Fear and risk plague leaders and result in less-than-optimal trusting decisions. When leaders delegate important tasks, they are doing their team members a favor, but they naturally worry that their team members will drop the ball. This leads them to trust less, to do more, and that negative spiral returns. Clearly, far too many leaders feel that "if you want something done well, you must do it yourself." This is a recipe for disaster, both for leaders and for their team members, who will feel alienated very quickly and become less productive. In sharp contrast, Do Nothing and Trust More is a dynamite combination.

This begs the important question of whether a leader's fears might actually have a rational basis: is it smart to be so fearful? Recent research data confirms my observations about eBay: leaders will miss some great opportunities if they act out of fear rather than taking the risks of trusting.

Clearly, leadership cannot exist without trust. People will not follow a leader they don't trust, and leaders won't get far if they don't trust people and delegate authority. When leaders don't trust their team members, they become micromanagers—by necessity. You only have two choices: you can trust or you will micromanage—particularly in the eyes of your team members, and the only people who want to be micromanaged tend to be brand-new, completely inexperienced team members.

Trust always incurs risk. Whenever you take a taxi, you trust the driver. This is an understandably scary thought. We do not trust because we are altruists: trust is not and should not be a gift. Instead, we trust for mutual benefit: leaders who trust team members who reciprocate and perform well benefit from having

trusted—and their team members benefit, too. Trusting More
wins for everyone.

It's ironic that fear actually feeds into the well-established, rational approach for leaders—to trust a person only minimally at first and to increase the risks of trust only gradually. When we don't know someone very well and we give them a small task, our actions reflect rationality based on fear—a strange combination. Rationality can also lead us to underestimate the value of second-hand information, like reputations, as well as ignoring the fact that people focus on how they've been treated when they choose how they will respond.

The fear that comes with trust should dissipate quickly with familiarity or with evidence. Leaders tend to trust people with critical tasks only when they know them very well. This makes no sense for leaders who have information about the people they can trust—even information from an impersonal, incomplete personnel file. Effective, *Do Nothing!* leaders trust people; they get over their understandable, rational fears quickly. They do their homework. They take business risks *and* interpersonal risks. They respect their team members and their professionalism, and they repeatedly follow another simple, two-word recommendation: they *Trust More*.

5

Release Control
(Deviously)

OHN WAS A very successful man. He had started his own company and it had grown and flourished. He was proud of his success and he was proud of the people who worked for him; he cared for them both personally and professionally.

One spring, during a relatively slow season for the business, he decided that he and his top management team, a group of twelve, would do a team development workshop. He had heard good things from colleagues about these kinds of ventures, and he felt that the company could be even more successful if his top lieutenants acted more as a team. So he signed them up for a workshop that was held outside a small town in Wisconsin. The facilities were fairly basic but the location was idyllic: hills, trees, lakes—simply beautiful landscape.

The centerpiece of the workshop was an outdoor challenge: an orienteering competition. Orienteering is a sport that focuses on running, strategy, navigation, and effective map reading. Individuals or groups are timed over a predetermined course that winds over or around lakes and hills through trees, forest, and open land. The goal is to quickly find a series of checkpoints that are shown on a map that the competitors receive at the starting line, right when their clock starts. World-class orienteering requires serious physical and mental skills, including strategic decision making.

For this executive team challenge, John and his group needed to traverse a challenging orienteering course as quickly as they could, as a team rather than as individuals. The workshop organizers showed them previous groups' record times; John and his top management team didn't need any more encouragement than this.

They were all well outfitted for the event: they had wet gear, boots, and provisions. The terrain in the area was challenging, with plenty of hills, trees, and wet areas.

Just before they began, they were all given topographical maps that indicated each of the checkpoints they had to find along their route. The clock started, and before anyone else could say anything, John looked up from his map and said, "I know where we're going. Follow me," and headed out.

He took a route that was a straight line from the starting point to their first checkpoint. As the crow flies, this would be the quickest way. Unfortunately, the map indicated that they might encounter a swampy area along the way. As they progressed, they did encounter a swamp.

This did not deter John at all. He kept right on going. He was well equipped with rubber boots, and his team was, too, so it looked like this might work.

As he charged ahead, however, his team started to slow down. The people whose boots were not as tall as John's were understandably concerned about filling them with cold water.

John sensed that people were not keeping up, so he looked over his shoulder, called everyone to "Come on!" and forged ahead.

He was not deterred when the water got deeper, and deeper, and deeper. Finally he heard a voice from among his team: "John, there might be a better way." He didn't look back but hollered over his shoulder, "No, this is the way to go!"

By this time, John was up to his knees in water. His boots were no longer functional. He finally looked back and saw all of his team standing still in almost knee-deep water. He did not want to turn back, but their demeanor told him that they weren't going any farther.

As it turned out, the best route to their first checkpoint required them to go around the swamp—which, at that time of the year, was actually a shallow lake. Although John was immensely determined to succeed, his strategy left more than a bit to be desired. In particular, he assumed that he knew what he was doing—in a completely new and unfamiliar situation—and didn't stop to consider the possibility that his highly qualified team members just might have some information or skills that would be relevant to their task. Instead, he thought he knew what to do and, even if he had been correct, he did far too much and left his team to do too little. (Remember, this was a team-building event.)

Democracy in Work Groups

All of us have been members of work teams. We have all experienced a variety of different leaders. They all have quirks; although John may be unusual and even unique, he is not outside the range of our experience of what's normal.

But let's think about democracy in work teams. Imagine one of those times when you were a member of a work team but you were not the leader. Almost all of the managers I meet indicate that, if they are not the leader of a team, they prefer that it be democratic. This is not a surprise, particularly because most of the time I'm interacting with managers in the United States, a country that identifies with democracy. But it's also true around the world.

Occasionally someone will indicate that they prefer that their work team *not* be democratic, and they have good reasons for this conclusion. Their foremost, best reason is that democracy is slow—an unassailable fact. If you have ever viewed an automobile accident, you know that it doesn't pay to jump out of your car, recruit all of the other nearby observers, and hunker down to make a democratic decision about what to do next. Instead, someone needs to take charge, to call for help, to make sure that the accident doesn't lead to another accident, and so forth. As Bob Cialdini notes in his wonderful book *Influence,* a person who takes charge and assigns people individual tasks that they need to do *now* can be tremendously effective.

But many work team tasks benefit most when *the team* makes the best possible decisions. Democracy may still not work best, however, if one member of the team has more expertise than anyone else. Then, democracy can dilute that person's expertise and lead the group to a suboptimal decision. So it makes eminent sense for experts to influence the group's final decision more than anyone else, albeit after seeking relevant input from other team members.

What do we mean when we talk about democracy in a work team? There are many definitions, including one person/one vote, equal influence, respectful consideration, and voice, that is, the willingness of other group members to listen to and seriously consider your ideas.

It's not difficult to narrow these definitions down. How many times have you been in a work team in which everyone has an equal vote? You may be smiling, because when I've asked executives this question, they smile, too: everyone having an equal vote is incredibly rare in work teams. Equal influence also doesn't happen much. Instead, organizations tend to be hierarchical structures that give some people more power and more influence than others, and everyone understands this. How this plays out from one situation to the next is critical, and different decision-making processes are needed in different situations. One size does not fit all.

Voice

Business schools are teams of students, faculty, administrators, and staff, all organized to provide a scintillating educational experience. Like any other team, it helps when they are well organized.

I once worked in a business school where the associate dean was the point person for every new idea; without his support, an idea had no chance of being considered. This made sense in terms of efficiency, with one person filling the essential role of gatekeeper. Any time anyone had a new idea, they made an appointment with the associate dean to get his support.

The first time I went, I was excited about my idea and presented it enthusiastically. He didn't ask me much about it; he paused for a bit, acting like he was considering it seriously, but in the end, he said no. I came away thinking that my idea might not have been so good. But the same thing happened the second time I brought him an idea. It happened the third time too. In fact, it continued to happen, every time I brought him another new idea. The only response I ever got was "No." It didn't take long for me to stop bringing him ideas. Obviously, this was pretty discouraging. But it also had more far-reaching effects.

During the time that he was dean, I could tell anyone who asked me exactly what my salary was. Normally I only remember my salary for about a week or two after I hear what it will be for the next year: I always have a general idea of what it is, but I don't know its exact value. But I did then.

Why? Well, it turned out that every time the school asked me to do something more than the strict requirements of my job, I asked myself, "Am I being paid enough to do this?" If the answer was "Yes," I would do the extra work; if the answer was "No," I wouldn't. This was not a happy period in my professional life. I particularly disliked the fact that I was constantly making these "Am I paid enough?" evaluations, but I couldn't get myself to stop.

When this associate dean stepped down and a new associate dean took over, I thought I'd try out my next great idea with him. To my great surprise, he seemed to listen carefully and, without even asking for more details, said, "Let's see if we have any money to pursue that."

I almost fell off my chair. I floated out of his office. The next morning, I did not need an alarm clock to wake up; instead, I was up early and off to the office, ready to go. More important, since that time, it's rare for me to be able to tell you what my salary is. Instead, when I have an opportunity to do something extra, there is no question; I just do it, and I'm much happier about it, too.

This is not an unusual story. People are more motivated when they have *voice*. Too many leaders act as if they don't realize this. Like John, they don't invite people to share their ideas and, even when people voice their ideas, they don't always listen carefully. These kinds of fairly subtle actions result in reactions that leaders truly don't want. In particular, like the story of the associate dean, having no voice is tremendously demotivating.

There are two key questions here: Do your team members feel like they have voice? Do they think that the team is democratic? It doesn't have to be democratic all of the time. When there's an emergency or a time crunch, everyone needs you to take over and be a directive leader. Also, when you are truly the team's expert on a task, you should be the most influential. But most of the time, your team members need to have voice to be motivated and effective.

Cardiac Surgery Teams

Let's take this a step further by considering some wonderful research by Amy Edmondson, a professor at Harvard. In one of her many interesting projects, Amy focused on cardiac surgery teams—work groups that need to be extremely well organized to succeed. These teams face high stakes; they have huge time pressure; they must coordinate themselves smoothly and effectively; and there is a wide range of skill sets within the team. Their leader is the cardiac surgeon; they also include an anesthesiologist, nurses (scrub and assisting), and perfusionists, who operate the heart-lung bypass machine.

During surgery, everyone on the team has a well-defined role, and everyone can see how things are going. They can also anticipate what they need to do next, pretty simply, by observing both the patient's heart and the surgeon's actions.

Amy's research focused on how cardiac surgery teams responded to a new surgical technique, minimally invasive cardiac surgery (MICS). Rather than opening up a patient's chest, MICS uses special equipment and small incisions between the patient's ribs to get to the patient's heart.

For patients, this is a tremendous improvement over the normally invasive procedure that opens up their chest cavity: MICS does much less damage to their body and their recovery time is less painful and much quicker. For the surgery team, however, MICS requires a three-day training program and an entirely different work routine.

MICS requires a huge increase in coordination. In particular, because the patient's heart is no longer open for everyone to see, the members of the team must now keep track of what is happening via monitors, and not everyone sees the same information on their monitors. In fact, each team member now has access to critical information that other members of the team may not have. This means that they must talk with each other, a lot. The team members now take on new tasks and different roles. Most important, people with less status must speak up more than they ever have before. As one of the anesthesiologists put it, "I have to be able to tell the surgeon to stop. This is very new. I would never have dared to say anything like that before."

Amy's research followed sixteen cardiac surgery teams in sixteen different locations. Although all of the teams found the new procedure to be truly challenging, some relished the challenge and others were discouraged by it. These reactions were directly related to their success. For instance, when team members felt hesitant to speak up, they were not as effective or as quick to implement this new procedure.

The more successful teams, in contrast, even found it easier to speak up in their training and practice sessions. This translated into the operating room.

Not surprisingly, the attitudes and actions of the cardiac surgeons, the teams' leaders, were critically important. Some surgeons took a radical approach, at least for them, by focusing on MICS as a truly *team* project. (This does not fit the common stereotype of the autocratic cardiac surgeon.) Some went so far as to acknowledge that their team's success depended on more than their own behaviors; in fact, it depended on the behaviors of everyone in the team. As one successful surgeon explained, "[This] is a paradigm shift in how we do surgery. . . . The whole model of surgeons barking orders down from on high is gone. There is a whole new wave of interaction. . . . The ability of the surgeon to allow himself to become a partner and not a dictator is critical."

Other signs of egalitarianism among the successful teams included the first invitations from surgeons to nurses and perfusionists to attend technical seminars. As an anesthesiologist noted, "This is a nonthreatening environment. It facilitates the flow of information." One of the successful teams was frequently visited by other teams. They had a "bring it on" attitude: as they put it, "It's amazing what you can learn from them if you listen. Even people who've just done a few cases have ideas."

Here we have very high status surgeons who have been trained to control the entire surgical process. They learn from medical school on that they are singularly responsible for the success of their procedures—even though they still need a team. They are also highly compensated and admired. It's no wonder that their colleagues characterize them as autocratic.

Their natural inclinations, however, can be disastrous with this new procedure because it requires them to release control, to depend on their team members, and to have and use voice and feel psychologically safe. In fact, it was only this kind of surgeon who could and would continue to use this marvelous new technique, which served everyone better, from the other members of the team to their patients. Not surprisingly, their experiences provide an important window into how all sorts of work teams can become more effective, and how their leaders can facilitate this process.

More Than Democracy

Have you ever had a question or an idea when you were working in a group, but you were afraid to raise it because you thought that someone might respond by treating you like a fool? Most of us have had this experience. We feel this way when we don't feel safe: we are afraid that our leaders or our colleagues will not consider our ideas and our questions at face value and respect us for asking them.

This is an issue that goes beyond democracy, and it is exactly the atmosphere that the best cardiac surgeons established in their MICS surgery teams. In Amy Edmondson's terms, the successful team leaders created an atmosphere that was *psychologically safe*: their team members could make observations; they could ask questions; they could comment on what they were seeing and they were encouraged to do so. This represents a truly radical shift for cardiac surgery teams.

Was everyone now of equal status in these groups? Obviously not. Everyone still accepted that the cardiac surgeon was the top gun. At the same time, however, everyone in the psychologically safe—and successful—teams knew that their ideas would be heard and respected, and that they needed to share them for the team to succeed.

This then begs another important leadership question: Do the members of your team feel psychologically safe? Can they ask a question or make a comment or even disagree—anytime? If not, they won't be as motivated as they might otherwise be.

It is up to you as the leader to make sure that your team members feel safe. You must bend over backwards to make this happen, because team members know that their leaders are always evaluating them and they have perfectly natural fears about the outcome of those evaluations. You must work doubly hard to help them feel safe: you must treat your team members' questions and observations as if you love hearing each and every one of them and you must entertain thier ideas and even invite them to disagree with you. You must make it eminently clear that you want them to participate, to question, to comment, and to disagree— and you need to reinforce them when they do.

Think of it this way: what would it be like if all of your team members felt that they had voice *and* that they were psychologically safe? This is an amazingly potent combination, one that results in people feeling like *owners*—like they truly have a stake in their team, their company, and their organization. This increases commitment and dedication, almost immeasurably. It's the kind of reaction that every leader wants.

Experience also indicates that it is extremely rare for any individual to repeatedly ask truly stupid questions. People do ask stupid questions now and again; that's natural. But competent team members don't do this repeatedly. So if you are going to make a leadership mistake, it pays to err on the side of voice and safety: if people have a natural tendency to stifle themselves and refrain from asking a question or making a comment, you will not get the kinds of critical information that can improve your team's decisions. Fearful silence can also lead to *pluralistic ignorance*—everyone having the same question but everyone simultaneously being afraid to ask it, and everyone missing out on information they need to perform well at their jobs.

Needless to say, pluralistic ignorance for a cardiac surgery team would be devastating, and maybe even fatal. It can have truly negative consequences for many other work teams too.

Amy Edmondson's research on cardiac surgery teams makes it eminently clear that leaders must work hard to create conditions of psychological safety for their team members; they must go out of their way to encourage questions, observations, and especially disagreement. People have a natural sense of uncertainty about their ideas: they can't be totally sure if they are on the right track or if they are way off. This sense of uncertainty can make them hesitant to interject—unless they know that their ideas and questions are *wanted and needed*. We all love to be needed—in work teams, it's up to you as the team's leader to make everyone feel comfortable, needed, and safe.

This is a particular challenge in tough economic times when people worry about being able to keep their jobs. The fear of a negative evaluation can reduce feelings of psychological safety and can limit an individual's willingness to speak up. To be as effective as they can be, however, your team members must feel that the team is democratic and that they are psychologically safe.

Control

But what about your natural inclinations as a team leader? Undoubtedly, the leader of any team is the person most responsible for the team and its outcomes. When we say that "the buck stops here," we mean that it stops at the feet of team leaders.

This leads to a natural reaction—taking control.

But in taking control, a leader necessarily reduces democracy. This creates what I call the Leadership Dilemma—a team of people who (1) want democracy and the opportunity for multiple inputs but (2) whose leader feels responsible, takes control, and reduces democracy. Both feelings are natural, but they are in direct conflict with each other.

Younger leaders are most affected by their natural tendency to want to take control. Think, for instance, of the first time you were promoted to lead a team. It is completely natural to want to show your new team members that you were promoted for good reasons and that it was the result of your skills, abilities, and potential rather than some sort of favoritism. Add to this the fact that, in many cases, people have been promoted over a current team member who also wanted the job, and their natural reaction is to take even more control and to immediately try to display all of their leadership skills (even if they don't have very many).

This can be devastating, because it can quickly and powerfully demotivate the team.

When a new leader is appointed, all of the members of a team become *hawks*—they are all anxious, watching intently because they want to know what their new leader will be like. They compare the new person's every word and every move to every leader they have ever encountered because any new leader is going to have a major impact on their lives.

When you were promoted to your first leadership position, it was for one of two reasons: (1) you were the most qualified person for the job; or (2) your bosses couldn't find anyone else. Either way, it doesn't pay to try to justify to your team members that you deserved the promotion. They know that you were promoted and that you will be their leader and that, if your organization's system is at least somewhat functional, you were promoted for one of these two reasons. Thus it pays for you to humbly accept your promotion, get on with the job, and not assume that you know more than everyone else.

The key is to create a democratic, trusting work environment that gives people voice and psychological safety. You can do this anytime, whether you have just been promoted or you have been leading your team for some time. People always appreciate the opportunity to share their ideas, and they all want the security that accompanies feelings of psychological safety. Encouraging your team members to have voice and making it clear that they are psychologically safe will mean that their lives will improve—maybe massively—even as it allows you to do less and be more effective. We all know how people react to leaders who are preening, autocratic, distrusting, dismissive, and domineering. They soon start wondering whether they should think about getting another position to avoid a truly uninviting work environment that weighs them down and reduces their effectiveness, every single day. This is not what you want your team members to feel.

Structural Control

So how to avoid the Leadership Dilemma? It is easy to say that you should not be controlling, that you should promote democracy and psychological safety, and that you should trust your team members, right from the start. All of these actions can be difficult to put into practice, but they will all help. Another old story also provides a glimmer of how you can establish feelings of democracy and safety within your team without completely releasing control. And yes, it is a bit devious.

When I was finishing school, I applied for faculty positions across the country and received a bevy of rejection letters. Finally, I got a job interview, at the University of Illinois; everything seemed to fall miraculously into place and they offered me the job. I can't describe how happy I was. But as I got my happiness under control, at least slightly, I couldn't help thinking that they must have made a mistake. Why in the world would they hire me? I didn't reveal these concerns to anyone, but I did worry about it.

We moved to Champaign, and shortly after we arrived an invitation came in the mail: to a welcome reception for new faculty members. This was awesome—I could go to the reception and see how much dumber I was than the other new faculty. If I was only a bit dumber than everyone else, I figured I could make up for it with hard work.

As it turned out, I had a great time at the reception because I wasn't much dumber than everyone else. I was extremely relieved: I actually had a chance to be successful.

I also met the president of the university, John Corbally, who was kind enough to attend. He was a very impressive person, and not just because he was the president of the ninth largest university in the nation, with sixty thousand students at three campuses (Urbana-Champaign, Chicago Circle, and the Chicago Medical

Center). He was also extremely articulate, seemed to be completely self-assured, and had "the look" of a great man. (In fact, after serving as president of the U of I for eight years, he became the first president of the John D. and Catherine T. MacArthur Foundation, which distributes millions of dollars to charities and research institutes, including its famous "genius grants" to help creative people pursue their work.)

I didn't want to monopolize his time, so I tried to ask him one question that I was truly curious about: "How is it that you have been so successful when most of the teams that you lead are composed of faculty members who have huge egos and want lots of control?" He smiled at my question, saying, "You're right; managing faculty members may be tougher than herding cats." But then he went on to say that every time he had a group or a team meeting, he created the agenda. Then he smiled again.

Let's think about this for a minute. He was suggesting, implicitly, that all he needed to do to retain control of people who wanted control was to create an agenda. Let's assume that he distributed his agenda a day in advance (always a good idea) or even just at the start of the meeting. When you have attended meetings that have an agenda, this is usually good news: it gives everyone an idea of the purpose of the meeting and it puts some structure around a process that can easily drift and not be particularly productive. (Do you look forward to meetings at work? Do you know anyone who does?)

The beauty of an agenda is that it gives the group members an opportunity to say whatever they'd like, as long as it conforms to the agenda. They can immediately feel that the process is democratic, particularly because an agenda doesn't seem like much of a constraint.

Here's the extra beauty of an agenda: by creating it carefully, a leader can retain more control than you might initially expect. Here's why.

When we make decisions, individually or as a group, we know that we should consider many alternatives and that we must narrow them down, gradually, until we reach a decision. Typically, we do this by eliminating alternatives that do not fit important criteria. But who's to say which criteria are most important and which we should consider first? If you want to be a leader who retains control, *you* should be the person to answer this question.

In fact, by structuring an agenda carefully, you can have a very good idea of which alternatives will be eliminated early in the process. If you understand the issues, the likely alternatives, the relevant criteria, and the inclinations of the members of the group, you can construct an agenda that eliminates, early in the process, the alternatives you don't want. The key insight here is that *eliminated alternatives are almost never reconsidered*. If leaders can create an agenda that eliminates the worst alternatives, the team can ultimately make a decision from among the best alternatives *and* feel that the process was democratic.

This is one example of what we call *structural control:* creating a structure (rules, processes, policies, etc.) that influences people even when you are not around. Clearly, there is deviousness in this process: you are letting people feel that the process has been democratic and that they have had voice, even though you have created it to subtly control the set of possible final outcomes.

Friedrich Nietzsche once said that madness is the exception in individuals but the rule in groups. So predicting a group's exact decision, however well you understand the problem, the criteria, the people, and the process, is still an uncertain undertaking. At the same time, a well-constructed agenda can help you to retain control; it can help the group reach a decision or move in a direction that you honestly feel is best for them and for the organization; and it can give them a sense of ownership in the process.

Structural control takes all sorts of forms. Incentive systems, for instance, are a perfect example of structural control: if you reward people more for moving east than you do for moving west, more people will move east, even when you are not present. It's natural.

Here's another example. I wrote my previous book, *The Art of High-Stakes Decision-Making: Tough Calls in a Speed-Driven World,* with a wonderful coauthor, John Mowen. John and I did a lot of research for the book, talking with people who made high-stakes decisions and trying to understand their decision-making processes as much as we could. Not surprisingly, I ask many of my students to read it, especially when my courses cover decision making.

When I teach in Kellogg's Executive MBA program in Canada, I'm there for two weekends, usually early and late February. In the first weekend, we have a class session on decision making—*before* I ask my students to read our book. Why? So that they can see what their natural tendencies are before they read about better ways to make their decisions. (By emphasizing interaction in our classes at Kellogg, we encourage self-discovery in the learning process. In this instance, learning increases when it follows self-discovery: people see the results of their natural tendencies first, as they are not always aware of them, and then they find out how to improve on them.)

After that class, I give everyone a copy of the book and ask them to read chapters 1 through 4 and 6 through 9, but *"Don't read chapter 5."* As you can imagine, the more I encourage them not to read chapter 5, the more tempted they will be to read it. So how can I encourage them to read the other chapters but not chapter 5?*

Structural control works wonders. In this case, before we give everyone their copy of the book, we staple chapter 5 shut.

---

*I don't want them to read chapter 5 because it reveals too much about an exercise that we do in our last class session. If too many people know too much about the exercise, it loses its impact. If only a few people know about it, it still works.

Obviously, it's easy to remove staples. (Similarly, when you put cookies or other temptations as far out of reach as you can, you can still reach them if you really want to.) But the staples, like the locks on the doors of our homes, act as an effective deterrent. (Truly dedicated burglars can overcome almost any lock, and truly curious people will take out the staples.)

Does it work? Extremely well: my final class exercise is always a stunning success. In other words, by using structural control and stapling chapter 5 shut, we have deterred most of the class from reading chapter 5, and the exercise shines.

Structural control can take many forms; it is a wonderful strategy for leaders. Organizational mission statements are another example of structural control: well-formulated, well-communicated mission statements help people make the right decision for their company, even when no one else is around. When you can set up a structure that influences people positively when you are not around, you become a more effective leader.

Circumventing Ulterior Motives

You might also think about using structural control when you need it most, such as when you know what is right for your team or your company but, because it will also give you great outcomes, people might think that you are only arguing to boost your own returns. This can happen, for instance, when you see a flaw in someone else's plan and you would benefit by having them change it.

You can solve this problem if you structure your meetings carefully. First start by asking yourself, if you don't want to be the one to criticize the plan, who can? The best critic is likely to be someone who is an expert and who has no ax to grind. If you can invite a respected colleague or two who have the appropriate skills and expertise—structurally controlling the composition of the group—and the flaw is sufficiently obvious, you need to do little more. If they need a bit of help to find the best solution, you should try to be as subtle as you can be. As we will see repeatedly throughout this book, you can also use a leader's most effective strategy: asking questions. Questions like "How would that work?" or "What would be the next step?" or "Who are the different groups that would be affected by this plan?" It is best, and most effective, if other people provide the answers—that way they can convince themselves, and you won't have to do the convincing.

Leaders in Action

Jack Welch and many other successful leaders are well known for constantly reiterating their company's goals. This is another way to use structural control. When Harry Kraemer talks about his tenure as CEO at Baxter International, he says that he spent 40 percent of his time repeating the company's goals and 40 percent of his time developing people. Although this meant that only 20 percent of his work time remained to do other things, his underlying logic is hard to dispute: if everyone is getting better at what they do and everyone knows what they want to achieve, it's highly likely they will achieve their goals.

In this sense, leadership does not have to be wildly complicated: make sure that people have voice; do all that you can to help them feel psychologically safe; set up structures that encourage them to do well and move in what you hope is the best direction possible. Then help them do that to the best of their abilities.

It doesn't have to be hard.

6

Bear Down Warmly

*N*ICE GUYS FINISH last. Although this old saying is often repeated, is it true? We can all think of anecdotes about people who are nasty but successful—for example, executives who have gotten nicknames like "Chainsaw Al" and who have moved from one executive position to another. But what about general trends? Should leaders be kind to their team members most of the time, or should they be tough? Should they be open to ideas or be directive? Should they delegate extensively or be sure they are always in control?

The answer to all of these questions is "Yes." Leaders must do all these things. In fact, leaders must be *wire walkers:* they must be able to walk a fine line between control and democracy, between delegation and taking responsibility, and between kindness and direction. Striking this balance is one of the biggest challenges that effective leaders face. Fortunately, there are solutions to this challenge, and research on effective leadership strategies gives us a host of hints about the nature of these solutions.

Researchers have been studying leadership for decades, and

the findings of each research study, in its own area, have been tremendously consistent. Over and over again, data indicates that leaders need to think carefully about two major issues, the task and the people. At the same time, however, a challenge comes from the fact that the findings on tasks and the findings on people are somewhat contradictory: effective leaders must push people to do more on their tasks and they must sincerely care about them at the same time. Neither requires that leaders do any work themselves, but determining how to combine the implications from the research on tasks and the implications from the research on people is not immediately obvious. Before we jump to conclusions, let's consider what each separate area of research tells us.

The Task

In terms of the task, the lessons are clear: to be effective, leaders must push people to do more than they otherwise would. Encouragement, high expectations, and a figurative but almost physical push can all help people achieve more than they would naturally expect or choose to do. People tend to be conscientious: they want to appear responsible and trustworthy, so when you give them a job, nearly all the time, they do it.

But then they stop. Only rarely do people do more than they are asked to do.

How can I make such a strong claim? Think of your own career. Think of the work that accumulates whenever you've been out of town and how you have called a meeting of your team members after your return so you could assign each of them a job to help you get caught up. When you do this, your team members do what you asked of them, but when they finish, they quickly return to their regular responsibilities. Only rarely do they ever do more.

In my own case, as a teacher, I've been assigning homework for years. One hand provides almost enough digits to count the number of times a student has done more than I've asked. Students don't do more homework than they are assigned—and, as a general rule, people don't do more work than they are assigned. (The nice exception is people who want to get ahead and move up the corporate ladder.)

If you want to be more effective, the conclusion from all this research is simple: ask people to *do more* than they otherwise would. They will not like you for this—no one wants to do more than they are comfortable doing or more than they are normally asked to do. This is the reason for the old saying "Leadership is lonely"; effective leaders push their people to do more than they otherwise would, and pushing people is not a great way to make friends. But to do really well, you must push your people to do more. If you don't, you will be stuck doing more than you should and, collectively, you and your team will accomplish less.

Sister Marie

When I was in the fifth grade, my teacher was Sister Marie Something—I remember the Marie part of her name but I don't remember her second name, and every time I think of Marie, I think of Antoinette and I know that's not right. So we'll just call her Sister Marie.

Shortly after the school year began, Sister Marie asked the entire class to work quietly at their desks on a set of math problems. While we were working, she asked me to come to the front of the room for a quiet conversation. She then proceeded to pull out several pages of math problems and told me that she'd like me to work on them and turn them in on Monday.

I was speechless. I was a shy ten-year-old, so it was not unusual for me to be quiet in the presence of adults and other authority figures, especially teachers. So although I only said, "Okay," I was stunned and less than pleased. When I got home that afternoon, I had several choice words to describe Sister Marie, albeit in the privacy of my own room. What was this all about? Extra homework? How is this fair?

Sister Marie proceeded to give me extra homework every week. Every week! This sparked one of my most verbally creative periods as a child. I created a series of incredibly succinct, brutal descriptions of her character. Boiled down to their essence, I concluded that she was mean, cruel, and completely unfair.

Although I was not fond of Sister Marie, I must also admit that, when I was a sophomore in high school and I was looking back at my life (all fifteen years of it), I realized that I had learned more math in fifth grade than I had in any other two years of school combined. Sister Marie was tough and demanding, but in retrospect, I couldn't help appreciating the fact that she pushed me: it made me better at math, a better student overall, and probably a better person. But this was *only* in retrospect. At the time, she was clearly acting as an effective, demanding leader—and I hated her for it.

Thus, we should revise the old saying: it should be "*Effective* leadership is lonely." You must push people to be successful—in fact, it's amazing how much a team can accomplish when they are pushed. There are many, many examples, including the following two.

#1—Door Fasteners

One of my recent executive MBA students told this story about his manufacturing firm. They make small fasteners that are used in the doors of cars, vans, and trucks. Because each door uses many of their fasteners, they make millions of them.

Although they are a regular supplier to all of the major

automobile manufacturers, one of their customers complained about the number of defects in their supply of fasteners. The company kept close tabs on this issue and realized that, out of every million fasteners they produced, an average of 1,500 had defects—in other words, they had 1,500 dpm (defects per million). Although 1,500 is a large number, 1,500 dpm is only .15 percent.

The firm wanted to be responsive to its customers, so it instituted a plan to cut down on defects. The company worked with its machinists to impress on them that this was important. It also installed a window assembly at each machinist's workstation. This gave the machinists a better, more immediate image of their ultimate goal: they weren't just trying to make a better batch of fasteners each day; instead, they were working on a critical element in a door assembly, which was a critical element in many vehicles, which were critical elements in transportation, which was a critical element in national and international commerce and in many people's lives. In other words, their manufacturing of small fasteners was a critical part of a bigger picture: they were facilitating people's social lives, interstate commerce, and many different modes of transportation.

This is a perfect example of using a superordinate goal to increase motivation: when people know that they are working for something more than just an immediate task, when they know that their ultimate goal is to help people and to improve how the world works, it's much more motivating, particularly when a task might otherwise be relentless, boring, and seemingly insignificant (or dirty work). This augments the important personal satisfaction of task accomplishment, which can now be even more rewarding.

The machinists' workspace improvements plus a substantive push to reduce defects led to continuous reductions in the number of defects in the company's fasteners. After a month, defects were down to 1,000 dpm. After another month, they were down to 500. Then 250, then 120, then 60, and so on. In fact, at the end of the eight-month program, they had reduced the number of defects *by 50,000 percent*, from 1,500 to just 3 out of every million fasteners.

Another way to look at this process: they cut their defect rate in half *nine times*. Imagine cutting your costs in half for a small task and then cutting them in half again and again, nine times. Imagine cutting the time it takes to do one of your team's important tasks in half and then cutting it again and again, nine times. This kind of improvement is amazing. Leaders who establish task-oriented environments where people take pride in their sense of accomplishment and who espouse a task-first, "let's worry about taking credit after we see how we do" atmosphere can approach their maximum potential—a state that is particularly, personally gratifying. Charles Schulz, the wise creator of the *Peanuts* cartoon series (first syndicated in 1950 and still running), had Linus say, "There's no bigger burden than that of having a great potential." This was a case of achieving that potential.

#2—Dental Work

I have had the opportunity over the last several years to work with leaders in many different fields; some of my favorites are the members of the American Dental Association. American dentists are becoming more entrepreneurial, and they don't get much leadership training in dental school, so Kellogg and the ADA have created a series of management programs, including what is essentially a mini-MBA.

Robert, one of the graduates of this program, told a lovely story about performance improvement that resulted from his attending a short workshop on a new, improved technique for installing a bridge. At the end of the workshop, the instructor encouraged everyone to try the new technique and, when they did, to time themselves. Then he suggested that, the second time they used the technique, they should *cut their time in half*.

Needless to say, many of the dentists at the workshop were skeptical: how could they maintain their high quality standards in half the time? (Note: Dentists really do want to do a great job fixing your teeth; the alternative is to cause you pain, force you to return to their office, and, as a result, consume time that they could use to treat someone else. Your and your dentist's incentive structures are completely aligned—a good thing for all of us.)

The instructor tried to assuage the participants' fears by indicating that he had cut his time in half, with no loss in quality, and he encouraged them to try it and to use the extra time to check the quality of their work.

Robert tried the new technique the first time he had a chance. It worked very well, a great improvement over his old technique. He also took care to time himself.

Because it went so well, the second time he used the new procedure he cut his time in half. To his surprise, quality was not compromised at all: it was just as good as it was the first time and continued to be an improvement over his old, standard technique. Every time he installed a bridge, he saved time *and* suffered no loss in quality.

Three weeks later, everyone who attended the workshop got an e-mail from the instructor, asking whether they had tried the technique, how it had gone, and whether they had cut their time in half. Robert responded positively to all three questions.

Three days later another e-mail came, summarizing everyone's responses. All of the dentists at the workshop had tried the technique and all of them had experienced positive results. In addition, everyone who had cut their time in half reported that they were still meeting or exceeding their previous quality standards.

After reporting these results, the instructor—who repeatedly demonstrated outstanding leadership—thanked everyone for having enough confidence to try this new technique. He also thanked the people who had cut their time in half. Then he encouraged the dentists who had not yet cut their time in half to try cutting their time in half, as their colleagues had already reported that it worked well. Then he encouraged the dentists who had cut their time in half to cut their time in half again.

Although Robert guessed that many of his colleagues continued to be skeptical, he had experienced such great success that, the next time he installed a bridge, he cut his time in half again. Then he carefully conducted a stringent quality check and, lo and behold, quality was just as good as before.

The obvious conclusion here is simple: we can do many, many things faster than we think we can. Speed-reading classes are all about reading faster without losing comprehension, and motivated graduates of these classes report amazing success—and huge time savings. Similarly, cooking classes train chefs to prepare food really quickly, with no loss in either quality or digits. The bottom line is that, on many tasks, people don't work as fast, often because they don't realize how quick they can be. Sometimes a leader just needs to give them a push—not only to help them streamline their efforts but also to force them to think of new, better ways to do their jobs. These are lessons that can extend to many tasks. By pushing people to do more, you can help your team members learn how to perform faster and cut their costs not just in one arena but in many, and, as a nice by-product, this allows you to do less and less.

The People

The second major finding from decades of leadership research is that leaders must *sincerely care* about their people. They must care about them as individuals; they must care about their careers; they must care about their families.

Here's the intuition: think of the great leaders you have known—I hope you have known several. My guess is that, whenever you encounter great leaders, you observe them carefully to determine what makes them great, as we all hope to emulate their style, their characteristics, and their strategies. If you notice all of the great leaders you have known do the same thing, you have probably discovered a great key to extraordinary success as a leader. In simple terms, if *all* of these great leaders are using the same tactic, it must be good.

My (bold) claim: when you think of the great leaders you have known, I'm willing to bet that all of them have had one common characteristic that you have *not* recognized. In other words, all of the great leaders in your life are alike in at least one respect, and you've missed it—even though you were probably conscientiously looking for it.

The answer? They all cared about *you* as a person. If they hadn't, they wouldn't be on your list of great leaders.

This means that, for you to be a great leader, your team members must know that you care about them. Jimmy Yaokasin was one of my executive MBA students in our program in Hong Kong; he put it this way: "People don't know how much you know until they know how much you care about them."* You could be the world's greatest expert on something, but if the people you work with don't know that you care about them, they won't listen to you much.

You should know your team members' birthdays, whether their parents are in good health, what their children are doing in school, and other important elements in their lives. The bottom line: you must get to know them personally. You don't need to

---

* This quote, or minor variations of it, has been attributed to many sources, some medical, some religious.

like them, but you must sincerely care about them. If you are not sincere, they will soon discover that you don't really care and that you're just acting like you do.

How much do you need to get to know them? Some leaders think they should adopt a formal role as a leader. This means that they act impersonally toward their team members because they think they need to maintain a distance and they shouldn't get too close. (Once again, this is the result of fear—in this case, the fear of having to tell someone you like that they aren't performing well.) So how do you balance your position of authority with your need to know them as people? Here's my standard rule, explained in an example: by all means socialize with your team members. Every so often take them out for a drink on a Friday afternoon. Talk about local community events, sports, the economy—you name it. You can even talk about work.

Buy them the first round. Also buy them the second round, but *don't* buy a second drink for yourself. Instead, take this as your time to leave. (Your timing does not have to be strict; this is just a general recipe.) Why? Most of the time, you should be the first person on your team to leave this kind of social event so that your team members can talk among themselves more comfortably.

You should also know that they want to talk about you, and nothing you do will stop them. Also, if you give them a golden opportunity to talk about you, with a drink in their hands that you have just purchased, the odds that they will say something positive about you go way up. You don't need to know every intimate detail of their private lives—far from it. But you do need to know them well enough to be able to socialize with them, comfortably.

The Balancing Act

How can you push people to do more but sincerely care for them at the same time? This is a conundrum, one of many that leaders naturally face. The solution to this problem is an old concept that is not discussed much these days: *tough love.* Tough love is caring enough about your people to push them to their maximum potential. In other words, set high goals for them and hope and expect them to fulfill your expectations without worrying about whether they like you.

This is what Sister Marie did for me; it's what they did in the Israeli army in the Pygmalion study; and it's what you can do for your team members. It also means that, in most situations, establishing true, reciprocal friendship is not possible. As Michael Abrashoff put it in *It's Your Ship:* "Being likeable is not high among a ship captain's requirements. What is essential is to be respected, trusted, and effective."

More on Great Leaders

If we tried to list all of the characteristics that are required of great leaders, the list could get really long—and no single person has ever been an expert at every aspect of leadership. Although you might ask yourself, "Where does this leave me?" the news is not bad. As noted in chapter 2, great leaders identify the team members who are most talented at a task and let them take over. As Abrashoff puts it, "No one person can stay on top of it all. That's why you need to get more out of your people," and "No one, including me, is capable of making every decision."

According to Abrashoff, people want just two things from a leader: support and respect. He also notes that friendship matters—you have to offer your team members your friendship even as you push them. What do you get in return? Not as much: your team members will almost never reciprocate your friendship completely. Instead, you must be like a benevolent dictator: it is critical for you to be kind, but it is not incumbent on your team members to reciprocate all of the favors that you provide.

Instead, you need your team members to think that you are and will act as their friend even if they don't want to be your friend and even when you must give them bad news. This is another reason why effective leadership is lonely.

The Bottom Line

The bottom line is clear: to be a truly effective leader, you must push people to do more; you must sincerely care about them as people; and you must be a *facilitator* and an *orchestrator*. They need to know that you care about them, even as you push them to do more. At the same time, you must help them to be able to do their jobs well and you must coordinate their activities so they can build on one another's efforts. As we've seen, one finger cannot lift a pebble, but you can act as the catalyst that helps everyone on the team thrive. You have to sacrifice to do this, by being more of a friend than they will be in return. This is just one of the tough realities of being an effective leader.

We don't naturally think of leaders as being facilitators. But here's a final bit of intuition: What if you practiced tough love successfully? More specifically, what would your life be like if all of your team members lived up to their maximum potential?

This question always leads to huge smiles on leaders' faces. The conclusion, again, is pretty obvious: help people do their jobs well and you can *Do Nothing!* Then add a bit of orchestration so that you start to hear symphonies more frequently. Once you get the hang of it, your job not only becomes much easier, but your team becomes much more effective.

7

Ignore Performance Goals

IT IS TIME for a contradiction. Or, to be kind, another conundrum. Performance goals are a task push, so they are an important part of every great leader's tactical toolbox. The problem is that leaders and their teams pay far too much attention to performance goals; as a result, they often lose sight of other equally or even more important goals, like the superordinate goals of the company or your own ultimate goals as a leader.

When an organization sets performance goals—say, cost reductions or performance achievements (sales targets, P&L gains, etc.)—people naturally pay a lot of attention because their evaluations, salaries, promotions, and bonuses typically depend on achieving these goals. Performance goals are best displayed as numerical targets—this makes their achievement measurable. Unfortunately, for many leaders, "hitting our numbers" can become all-consuming, especially as deadlines approach.

As noted in chapter 3, workplace scholars have long known that performance goals should have three characteristics: they should be measurable, schedulable, and accountable. In other words, a specific person or team should achieve a clear target by a particular time. This results in goals that are both unambiguous and noteworthy: they push people to pay attention to how they are progressing toward the goal and achieving the desired outcome. Well-specified, numeric performance goals, however, not only don't encourage consideration of other critical aspects of your work team's process, they can crowd out less specific but more important goals—and this is where the trouble lies.

A sports example shows why. Imagine that you are with a few friends on a beautiful day, playing golf. You went to the course early to stretch and hit a few practice balls before you began. As you were driving to the course, you anticipated what might happen: you were hoping for a good score; it was great to be getting away from the rat race; golf courses are a great place to commune with nature; and you loved the idea of getting some fresh air and exercise and hanging out with your friends. In other words, before you started, you hoped that your day at the course would achieve a variety of different goals.

Your round started out well and, after finishing the first four holes, you realize that your score is superb—far better than normal. You always compare how you are doing to par (a common golf standard) and to your normal score, so you can't help thinking that this could be a special round. As a result, if you are like most golfers, you naturally shift your focus to achieving a great score, maybe even a personal best, and your other goals—getting away from the rat race, communing with nature, getting some fresh air and exercise, and hanging out with your friends—quickly fade into the background. In other words, your performance goal has now become both dominant and much more specific. Because it is so outcome-oriented, all of your motivations now focus on one thing: your final score. You are playing well and all you need to do is keep it up.

What is the natural result of this all-too-common process, both immediately and for the rest of the round? If you are like most golfers, your performance will immediately crumble—all those good things you had been doing well quickly disappear and your score balloons, sometimes to the point where you actually do worse than normal, even given your wonderful start. Shifting your focus to a hoped-for performance outcome has, paradoxically, made it almost impossible for you to achieve it.

This is not true of every endeavor; many times—particularly for routine tasks—an increase in effort and sharpened concentration lead to better performance. For tasks that require tremendous mental concentration, however—like golf—increasing your outcome orientation can be devastating.

Tasks that require a strong cognitive focus and the application of a strong intellect are exactly the kinds of performance contexts leaders typically face. But focusing on your final outcome can be deadly—it substitutes specific, outcome-oriented, short-term goals for broader, superordinate, long-term goals. At the extreme, it can shift your attention away from the central reasons why you are doing what you are doing to something more mundane, more immediate, and, in the end, far less satisfying.

Performance Goals Disappear

This is not to say that we should completely do away with performance goals; they still have tremendous value as a task push. Instead, it is critical to keep them in perspective so other important goals still get our attention as well.

Let's assume that you continue to use performance goals to help your team hit your targets and then let's consider how this process naturally plays out. First, what happens when you and your team have achieved a performance goal? In most cases, *it disappears*. What happens next? It is almost always replaced, immediately, by a more challenging, more difficult goal.

Most people can't remember their old performance goals, not even from as little as three years ago. In other words, they truly, completely disappear. Not only that, when I ask leaders whether they ever get performance goals that get *easier* over time, they laugh—it's pretty much unheard of.

This means that people pay a lot of attention to goals that quickly disappear from their memory and each previous goal is quickly replaced by a new, tougher goal. This process repeats itself over and over. In economies that focus on quarterly reports, this can happen as often as every three months, with the higher-ups in the company continually emphasizing that hitting your numbers is absolutely critical. Situations like these naturally focus people's attention far too much on their performance goals, leading them to neglect other critical goals, especially the less well-specified goals that may not naturally garner as much attention. In particular, by paying attention to performance goals, leaders often lose complete sight of their *learning goals*.

Why are learning goals so important? The logic in answering this question is straightforward and unassailable: if you and your team's abilities stay the same and you continuously face increasing performance goals, pretty soon you will not be able to achieve them. Thus, as your performance goals increase, so must your ability. When you focus too much on performance goals that interfere with your attention and your devotion to achieving your learning goals, you are bound for failure: how soon is a function of how much your performance goals increase each time they change, how able your team is now, and whether those new goals require skills that you and your team may not yet have. The bottom line is simple, but not something that leaders naturally notice: you must continuously boost your ability, and the only way to do that is to continuously focus on learning, on getting better, on knowing more. It's the only way to consistently achieve an ever-increasing sequence of performance goals.

"Leaders Are Born, Not Made"

"Lifelong learning" is a common catchphrase at business schools. It is a goal that many dedicated educators embrace and deeply believe in. (It also has extra, added value: if we can convince people that it is necessary and worth achieving, it will keep our classrooms full and us employed.)

Whenever learning is on the agenda, people ask a basic, important question: whether leaders are born or can be made. Most people believe that leaders are born and, if they weren't, it's almost impossible for them to learn to become really great leaders.

This is an old argument—and frankly, it's hogwash. People are amazingly adept at learning and they can keep on learning even as they get older. Not only that, with the world changing as it does, people with different backgrounds can now succeed in ways we never before contemplated. It wasn't very long ago, for instance, that someone like Bill Gates would be ostracized at school: geeks were definitely not cool. Now they are at the forefront of our ever-expanding technological world, and their inventions have created all sorts of new needs that only they can satisfy.

There's another huge downside to believing that leaders are born and not made: all you need to do is buy into this belief and it will justify mediocrity, laziness, and the Peter Principle, that is, the idea that people tend to rise to their level of incompetence. Although the Peter Principle fits our observations of many leadership failures, Dr. Laurence Peter and Raymond Hull used anecdotal observations to formulate their central concept, which they presented for the first time in 1969. To date, there is no hard empirical evidence to suggest that it happens to everyone (as some have argued). It makes for a catchy story but it can't explain the legion of outstanding CEOs around the world.

Also, anyone who has repeated contact with motivated leaders who are always looking for ways to get better can see how leaders grow and actually get better over time. Personally, I've seen it happen many, many times.

Why do people believe that leaders are born, not made? It may be because psychologists long ago suggested that people were born with a fixed supply of intelligence and that nothing they could do would ever change it. Old data also suggested that our intelligence diminished over time—that we peaked in early adulthood and then gradually got dumber as we got older.

The tests that led to this conclusion, however, had a fatal flaw. In the early days of intelligence testing, it was impossible to measure someone's intelligence when they were young and then follow them and retest them repeatedly as they got older: there wasn't enough time or financial support for this kind of research, and it was hard to stay connected to the same group of people to be able to test them repeatedly. To evaluate the relationship between intelligence and age, early intelligence researchers compared the average scores of eighteen-year-olds with the scores of thirty-six-, fifty-four-, and seventy-two-year-olds, with everyone taking the same test. These studies showed that older people's scores were, on average, lower than younger people's scores. This led to the conclusion that as we get older, we get dumber.

It turns out, however, that IQ scores have increased across generations: being born more recently means that, on average, your test scores are likely to be higher than they were for people born years before you. James Flynn's research has shown, for instance, that, in fourteen countries, IQ scores show consistent gains across generations (see Figure 1 for data on five of those countries). Not only are we likely to know more than our ancestors did because we are generally more educated than they were and because more is generally known now than was known then, but it also appears that we are smarter, at least in terms of IQ scores, than they were.

Although memory fades and older people are not as well equipped to answer IQ test questions quickly—which does not help their scores—it is not at all clear that we get dumber as we get older. On many facets of an IQ test, people's scores actually tend to increase as they get older. Our children may not agree—remember Mark Twain's observation: "When I was a boy of fourteen, my father was so ignorant I could hardly stand to have the old man around. But when I got to be twenty-one, I was astonished by how much he'd learned in seven years"—but we may be getting smarter rather than dumber as we get older. If so (and there is some controversy and a lot of complexity that makes this

FIGURE 1. IQ GAINS OVER A FIFTY-YEAR PERIOD IN FIVE COUNTRIES

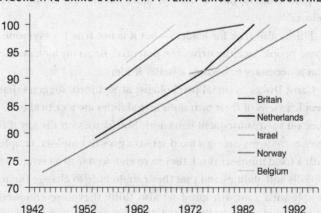

Adapted from James R. Flynn. "Searching for Justice: The Discovery of IQ Gains over Time." *American Psychologist* 54 (1999): 5-20.

a difficult question to answer), it also means that environment plays a strong role in determining our IQ scores, especially when we consider that we ourselves are able to influence our own environments. People who constantly give themselves intellectual challenges continuously create great environments for themselves and give themselves opportunities to boost their IQs as they get older.

Alfred Binet, the creator of the first intelligence test, also rejected the idea that our IQs are fixed. He developed the IQ test to identify children who were not keeping up intellectually so that programs could be designed to help them. Although he was obviously aware of the reality of individual differences, his conclusions were strong and clear: "A few modern philosophers assert that an individual's intelligence is a fixed quantity, a quantity which cannot be increased. We must protest and react against this brutal pessimism. . . . With practice, training, and above all, method, we manage to increase our attention, our memory, our judgment and literally to become more intelligent than we were before."

This is also true for leaders—but it is not true for everyone. Some people lack the drive, the potential, or an outlook on life that is necessary to become a better leader.

Carol Dweck, a social psychologist at Stanford, suggests that people's views of their own skills and abilities are a critical influence on their subsequent behaviors. She focuses on the key difference between having a fixed versus a growth mind-set: people with a fixed mind-set think they were endowed with a certain set of skills and abilities and that they can do little to change them; people with a growth mind-set also think they were endowed with a certain set of skills and abilities but they believe they can grow and improve. Her work with children on learning and performance goals contributes directly to the ideas in this chapter, as she has shown that kids who focus too much on performance run into trouble, whereas kids who focus on learning continually strive, even in the face of adversity, and grow.

Dweck and others have also found that our mind-sets can be influenced and changed. People who have a fixed mind-set can learn to adopt a growth mind-set and, after this change, can alter their subsequent behaviors in particularly positive ways. This can be critical for leaders, as our mind-sets have an important impact on how we approach problems and how we pursue our goals.

How can you help people accomplish this shift?

Dweck's research has shown that praising a successful child *for her efforts* is much more effective at increasing her subsequent motivation than praising that same successful child for her intelligence. This way she learns to work hard rather than to sit back and depend on her skills to help her succeed. Dweck's research has also measured the effects of different mind-sets on people's brain waves (via an EEG) while they answered a series of trivia questions. Her participants had to wait one and a half seconds before they learned whether they were right or wrong, and, if they were wrong, another one and a half seconds before they learned the correct response.

She found that during those waiting times, people with fixed mind-sets cared a lot about whether they were right or wrong but cared less about what the right answer was. In contrast, people with growth mind-sets wanted to know the correct answer and were less concerned about validating their own intelligence. In addition, when they had an opportunity to retake the same test right away, the growth mind-set people learned from the experience and performed better, but the fixed mind-set people did not.

More generally, Dweck has shown that people with fixed mind-sets focus more effort on showing how smart or how talented they are rather than trying to develop themselves. As a result, they tend to scoff at the notion that effort matters.

Allen Iverson's reactions at a press conference, after his Philadelphia 76ers team lost in the first round of the 2002 NBA playoffs to the Boston Celtics, are a perfect example. When a reporter
asked him to comment on his coach's criticism of his lack of devotion in practice, he reacted incredulously, derisively repeating
the word *practice* more than twenty times. At the end of his extended rant, he was still incredulous at the idea that practice
might be important: "How the hell can I make my teammates
better by practicing?"*

If Iverson had read some of Carol Dweck's research, he would
have had a neat, clear answer: with a growth rather than a fixed
mind-set, he might have realized that his immense skills—and
his connections with his team members—could have gotten even
better if he had been more dedicated in practice. He was an immensely talented basketball player, but he seemed to be overly
impressed by what he could do—not a surprise when you consider how he was fawned over from the time he was a kid. But it
is exactly that kind of fawning attention, *to talent rather than effort*,
that can warp children's outlooks and misdirect their motivation
and ultimate direction in life.

Applying this research to leadership suggests that leaders with
fixed mind-sets will worry about how adequate they are: they will

---

* The full quote: "We're sitting here, and I'm supposed to be the franchise player,
and we're talking about practice. I mean listen, we're sitting here talking about
practice, not a game, not a game, not a game, but we're talking about practice.
Not the game that I go out there and die for and play every game like it's my last
but we're talking about practice man. How silly is that? . . . Now I know that I'm
supposed to lead by example and all that but I'm not shoving that aside like it
don't mean anything. I know it's important, I honestly do but we're talking about
practice. We're talking about practice man. We're talking about practice. We're
talking about practice. We're not talking about the game. We're talking about
practice. When you come to the arena, and you see me play, you've seen me play
right, you've seen me give everything I've got, but we're talking about practice
right now. . . . Hey I hear you, it's funny to me too, hey it's strange to me too but
we're talking about practice man, we're not even talking about the game, when it
actually matters, we're talking about practice. . . . How the hell can I make my
teammates better by practicing?"

focus far more on *show* and not enough on *grow*; they will trumpet the goals that they have and that they will achieve and ignore the fact that they are treading water and not getting better. Not only that, their promises of future goal achievement will necessarily fail, as external standards keep moving up and a leader's abilities must move up just to keep up. The results of this orientation can be so severe—and they were in one study—that children with a fixed mind-set were more likely to lie about their performance on a test than were kids who had a growth mind-set. The reason? They had to show people they were smart, even if they had to lie to do it. Parents of teenagers have often seen this kind of self-consciousness interfere with their kids' abilities to mature, to learn, and to get a sense of satisfaction in striving. Thankfully, many teenagers outgrow this—but some don't, and they needlessly suffer because of it. Although I'm not a psychoanalyst, I can't help observing that they even seem to be less happy in life than they might otherwise be.

Would adults with a fixed mind-set also lie? We don't know yet, but research on the effects of fixed and growth mind-sets has started to emerge for adults. Laura Kray and Michael Haselhuhn, for instance, recently studied the effects of mind-sets on performance in a negotiations course. They found that people with a growth mind-set were less likely to see negotiations and conflict in black-and-white, winner-loser terms, and more likely to think that cooperation among conflicting negotiators was possible. In a second study, after reading either an essay titled "Negotiation Ability Is Changeable and Can Be Developed" or one titled "Negotiation Ability, Like Plaster, Is Pretty Stable over Time," the people who read the "Changeable" essay were much more likely to choose a task where, although they would "make a bunch of mistakes, get a little confused, and maybe feel a little dumb at times," they would eventually learn some very useful negotiation skills; they also achieved negotiation outcomes that were almost twice as good as the outcomes that people who had read the "Plaster" essay had negotiated. Growth mind-set people were also almost twice as likely to discover creative solutions that turned a tough, seemingly hopeless negotiation into a mutually beneficial agreement. The growth mind-set MBAs even got higher overall grades in the course.

A 6-STEP PLAN TO ENCOURAGE LEADERS TO ADOPT A GROWTH MIND-SET

1. Read a scientific report indicating that skills and talents are not fixed. (Or view a video illustrating how the brain is capable of "growing like a muscle" throughout life.)
2. Write down at least three reasons why it is important for a manager to realize that people can develop their abilities, including implications for both you and your team members.
3. Reflect on situations when you and other people you know have changed and developed their abilities and personalities over time.
4. Write an e-mail to a hypothetical protégé describing evidence that abilities can be developed and add an anecdote or two about how you have overcome professional development challenges.
5. Identify (a) three times when you saw someone learn to do something they thought they could never do, (b) why this occurred, and (c) how their doubt might have influenced their potential.
6. Share your responses to #5 and #6 with two other people who share their responses with you.

Adapted from the work of Peter Heslin and his colleagues.

Effective leaders need to negotiate well, and these data suggest that a growth mind-set is directly related to this critical skill. Other research by Peter Heslin, a professor at Southern Methodist University's Cox School of Business, and his colleagues has shown that team members perceive managers with a growth mind-set as better coaches than managers with a fixed mind-set. In addition, the growth mind-set managers themselves indicated a greater willingness to coach their employees than fixed mind-set managers did. Most important for our purposes, Heslin and his colleagues have found that people with a fixed mind-set can be taught to become more growth minded in less than a twelve-step program. (Only six steps are needed [see the chart on the opposite page], and all six can happen right after one another—the process does not need to be drawn out.) Early findings also suggest that these changes endure.

Everyone starts with opportunity: some people start with more, others with less. Although being blessed with a great genetic structure, strong parents, and a supportive developmental environment certainly helps, achieving greatness as a leader also takes diligence, learning from experience, constantly seeking information and insights, and making the effort to grow.

Robert Sternberg, another psychologist and a renowned expert on intelligence, summarizes this approach beautifully: he suggests that expertise results primarily from "purposeful engagement." I've always focused on the related concept of *perseverance*, and I try to pronounce it as Nina Hatvany pronounces it: per-*sev*-r-ens, with the accent in the middle. Nina got her PhD in psychology from Stanford and went on to teach at Columbia's and Berkeley's business schools. She then left academia and has established herself as one of the top real estate agents in the San Francisco area.

Nina's dissertation was about the perseverance of information. When we met, our conversation ranged widely and, ever since, I have often thought of the more general concept of perseverance—because of her interesting pronunciation. Perseverance is particularly important for academic success: professors are generally pretty smart people, and some are remarkably intelligent. How can anyone stand out and succeed in such a smart crowd? It often comes back to perseverance (per-*sev*-r-ens): people who can get past the intense criticism and the seemingly endless series of professional obstacles in academia are the ones who come out on top in the end. My guess is that it has been a critical part of Nina's enormous success as a real estate agent as well.

Molding Your Team

You do not want to be the only leader on your team. When you give people authority to do a task on their own, you want them to step up and take on the role of being a leader. How can you accomplish this, in addition to the laudable act of giving them discretion and authority on tasks in which they are experts? You can work on their mind-sets, on how they approach problems.

By adopting a growth mind-set, people see that effort, not show, is critical. *The New Yorker* ran a story that was a perfect example several years ago: it focused on the joy of mediocrity. The story described an amateur saxophone player who was not and never would be a great musician, however hard he tried. At the same time, he loved every opportunity he had to play. In fact, he loved it so much that it made other people happy to watch him (because his playing was not painful—it just wasn't great). As a result, he was a sought-after (and inexpensive) wedding musician because all he wanted to do was play the sax and make people happy.

Carol Dweck's research makes it clear that almost all of us have more potential than we ultimately achieve. Her findings present a particularly optimistic view of life, giving everyone hope that they can be effective leaders. It may not be true for everyone, but the possibility is out there for those who want to try. As she points out, "Darwin and Tolstoy were considered ordinary children . . . Ben Hogan was completely uncoordinated and graceless as a child . . . and the renowned photographer Cindy Sherman . . . failed her first photography course."

The key element for leaders is that, rather than focusing only on performance goals—a means of showing the world your talents—you also need to focus on learning goals. Imagine the converse—a supervisor who is stuck in a fixed mind-set. It is easy to imagine this person being controlling or even abusive, and when this happens, team members will also feel compelled to adopt a fixed, we-better-perform mind-set. The natural result is little if any attention to learning, and as demands increase, this approach is ultimately defeating. As Dweck puts it, "It's hard for courage and innovation to survive a company-wide fixed mindset."

Promoting a growth mind-set can even be true of entire organizations. Glen Tullman, the increasingly successful CEO of Allscripts, has a philosophy that supports almost any kind of education, for anyone. In their performance reviews, he asks his people to report any and all education experiences they have had—and they are rewarded for all of them.

Why such a blanket plan? What if people are learning how to be sword swallowers or belly dancers? How could that help a health-care company? Glen's philosophy is simple: you never know. The world is changing so quickly that you can't anticipate the skills you will need, or which skills might transfer to new situations. In addition, a general, overarching push to get more education is likely to have all sorts of positive spillover effects: expanded domains for curiosity, greater overall feelings of accomplishment, and a boost to individuals' feelings of self-efficacy. It also helps to create more interesting people who might look forward to coming to work with one another even more than they did before. They might even be more committed to the company.

All of this focuses on *attitude:* how we feel about who we are and what we do. Converting attitudes into behavior is not always either direct or easy: charitable people don't always contribute;

honest people sometimes tell white lies; and religious people don't always attend church. Another challenge for you as a leader is to convert your team members' (and your own) positive attitudes into positive behaviors that facilitate learning. Here's how.

No More Postmortems

Let's think about work as if it were encapsulated—for example, project work, with a clear beginning and a clear end. Let's also describe work as a set of projects even though, for many people, it might be a continuous process.

Here is the critical question: after every project, do you consistently convene what I call a Post-Project Evaluation Meeting? (These used to be called postmortems.

Post-Project Evaluation Meetings (PPEMs) are simple meetings that don't require a lot of time: their benefits-to-costs ratio is enormous. They also have a simple, four-point agenda:

1. What did we do well?
2. What did we do poorly?
3. What surprises did we encounter?
4. What can we do better?

That's it; a simple agenda, a quick meeting, and you and your team members have started an important, self-propelled internal learning program. The obvious goal is to repeat what you have done well, avoid repeating what you have done poorly, anticipate what was a surprise, and think of new ways to improve. These meetings can be remarkably effective.

Two caveats: Caveat #1—People who are not used to these kinds of meetings are often reluctant to discuss their mistakes in a public forum, especially one that you, their leader, is attending.

Who wants to remind everyone what they did wrong? Most people naturally want to bury their mistakes. So if these meetings are a new experience for you and your team, it is up to you to get things started: you must take the lead by openly discussing your own mistakes. This way you can set the tone and you can encourage other people to follow. It usually helps to do this at the start of every meeting; it can also help if you reward people for sharing their mistakes. (It would be devastating to punish them, as this will quickly kill the potential effectiveness of these meetings.)

Will this be easy? We've already discussed in chapter 4 the fact that many leaders find it difficult to apologize. Apologies are not part of PPEMs. Instead, everyone must simply air what they did wrong so that everyone in the team can learn from one another and not make the same mistakes twice. PPEMs are all about information; they are not meant to be confessions or blame-taking sessions.

One of my recent executive MBA students and his team have become masters at PPEMs. One member of his team brought a large ceramic bust of Elvis Presley to the office and awarded it to the person who had made the biggest mistake on their last project. This is a truly ugly sculpture, but it is displayed with great honor and fanfare on the winner's desk, and after every PPEM, it moves to the desk of the person who has made the latest big mistake. As my exec student noted, Elvis has become such a sought-after trophy that, instead of wanting to sweep their mistakes under the rug, every member of his team campaigns to win Elvis. It works beautifully (with good humor, too).

Caveat #2—If you implement Post-Project Evaluation Meetings, you must be sure to follow through so that the ideas you raise in your meetings actually have an impact on your team's subsequent behavior. It is pointless to hold these meetings and then not benefit from them. Publicizing the results and publicly rewarding people who implement the great new ideas you have learned or those who avoid making a previous mistake goes a long way toward institutionalizing the learning that you can obtain from a PPEM.

An Equation

As a leader, you can control the work process, but you can't control its outcomes. There are thousands of examples. For instance, you might ask one of your team members to prepare a sales presentation to a potential new customer. She can do a remarkably good job preparing and presenting your case, to the point of getting a standing ovation from the customer's evaluation team—and they still might give the contract to one of your competitors.

> *You can't control the wind, but you can adjust your sails.* (Yiddish)
>
> *Pray to God, but row for shore.* (Russian)
>
> *There is no bad weather, only bad judgment.* (Kiwi)
>
> *It's better to light a candle than to curse the darkness.* (Chinese)
>
> *Trust in Allah, but tie your camel.* (Arabic)

In other situations, bad luck might overcome all of your best efforts. You might have the world's best idea for a new product, service, or company, for example, but rather than investors lining up to give you money to get things going, the economy crashes and credit is not available—for anyone. Your idea was great but your timing was wrong, and that's enough to sink a great idea.

The simple moral to these stories is that, as a leader, you can do everything possible to control the process—you can assign tasks, you can establish deadlines, you can monitor your group's progress—you can do everything right, but you still can't control outcomes. Coaches in sports know this only too well: they can get the very most out of their players and still lose.

We can depict this truism in the form of an equation:

Outcomes = *f*(Ability + a lot of other stuff)

In words, every outcome is a function of two things: ability plus a lot of other stuff, and other stuff always happens. Every wise leader knows that, however well you elaborate your plans, however thoughtful and careful you have been, your pre-action outline of what you think will happen only remains intact until the moment you begin implementation. Then things almost always change, usually by necessity. As the saying goes, "the best-laid plans of mice and men" almost never go as planned.

I've had the good fortune, on several occasions, to interview professional negotiators. I often ask them how many times they have had a negotiation go exactly as planned. Their response is almost always a smile, followed by the same explanation: "My plans never work out as I had hoped. Something always goes wrong."

In other words, stuff happens. As a leader, you must prepare for it, cope with it, and move forward. You must be flexible in your means and keep your eye on your ultimate goal. Most of all, you must facilitate your team members' skills and performance—including their ability to act as leaders themselves—so they can handle crises without you. Remember, your plans are not important on their own, they are only important in helping you to achieve your goals. If they are not working, don't hesitate—change your plans and keep seeking that goal.

This also means that you shouldn't focus on outcomes so much. Focus instead on doing things right, on the best possible process, and on paying attention to what you can do rather than to what you can't control. We can take our pick of many proverbs (see above) to see that this is a basic truth.

The Finale

The bottom line: don't just focus on your performance goals. Even if you achieve them, you may miss much more. Effective leaders achieve far more when they focus their attention on learning and ignore performance goals, which will almost always be around and which require almost none of your attention to still have their desired impact. Instead, it is far more important to focus on what is less natural: learning. It is all too easy to let learning be forgotten or pushed aside by too much attention to performance goals.

Once again, the solution here is easy: facilitate a growth mindset in your team members so that they can grow. As your collective abilities increase, positive outcomes will naturally follow, and you can do less and less.

De-emphasize Profits

YOU'RE TO BLAME for the recent financial meltdown."

How's that for an accusation to make you pause?

I was at O'Hare Airport, waiting for a flight to Miami and worried about whether the Chicago weather would let us take off.
Who do I run into in the waiting area but Michael Krasny, the
founder and ex-CEO of CDW (Computer Discount Warehouse),
an immensely successful company that sells computers, computer
systems, printers, software, accessories, and the like. It was Michael who leveled that accusation at me.

I had met him several years ago when I coordinated a week-
long leadership workshop for CDW's top one hundred people.
We had many occasions to talk and, as a sales-oriented entrepreneur, Michael was very good at telling a story. His own personal
story is wonderful.

His father was a car salesman who, in his early years, was not
particularly ethical. Bait-and-switch was one of his favorite ploys:
advertise a car at a very low price and, once a customer has gotten

excited about buying it, "realize" that the car actually has several extra options and the actual price will be much more than expected. Michael was careful to note that his father wasn't very successful until he opened his own dealership and decided to change his ways.

Michael was a keen observer and realized that treating people well was a good idea, not only for its own sake but for its positive effects, too. He also had the bug to be an entrepreneur. After trying a few career paths that didn't pan out, he took a computer programming class, "the first time I was ever a star pupil. I absolutely loved it." Nevertheless, when he ran short of cash, he decided to sell his computer. He sold it quickly and, during the process, "someone else came along and said they would have liked to have bought it. So I said that I would get them another one." After buying another used computer and selling it to him, Michael realized that selling computers might be a good business. Not only that, it would be a perfect way to combine his entrepreneurial spirit with his passion for technology.

Before long, he was selling fifty to one hundred computers a week out of the back of his trunk and his garage. He was twenty-eight years old. Twenty-four years later, in 2006, CDW had 5,640 coworkers and more than $6.8 billion in sales.

Why was he so successful? Obviously, many factors contributed. As he puts it, "There is no secret sauce, but there is a recipe. The recipe consists of equal parts of a) great coworkers who care, b) loyal customers, and c) execution." (More on Michael in the next chapter.)

The Economy

Was I really to blame for the crash of the world economy? Thankfully, Michael quickly admitted that he did not blame me as an individual. Instead, he was blaming business schools that pushed the goal of maximizing profits rather than maximizing value. But was he right? Was profit maximization the driving force behind the collapse of the global economy? It would not be hard to make a strong argument to support this idea.

Focusing just on the United States reveals that the stock market was riding high in late 2007. The Dow Jones Industrial Average hit its peak on October 9, 2007, when it closed at 14,164.53. Less than a year and a half later, on March 9, 2009, it had plummeted to 6,547.05, a drop of 53.8 percent. The entire world economy was reeling. Here in the States, people who were looking forward to retiring saw their retirement accounts lose 40 percent of their value, or more. Immense (paper) wealth just went up in smoke and thousands of people lost their jobs.

Many analysts who have reflected on the events prior to the crash have noted that the seeds of the crisis were sown in the housing market in the mid-nineties when the federal government launched an effort toward what seemed like a laudable goal—pushing for more Americans to be able to own their own homes. The problem with this idea, of course, was that many Americans simply didn't have enough money to afford their own home.

Unfortunately, mortgage lenders embraced this goal, and subprime loans were born. Then, before you know it, they went viral, as did home equity loans. When home values rose, more and more people took out home equity loans. Financial wizards then created new derivatives to bundle subprime loans and sell them in the financial markets, and everyone was profiting, sometimes massively—until home prices stopped rising and the crisis began.

How could a leader, or a business school, have stopped this massive movement? Michael Lewis, in *The Big Short*, noted that banks had always known that people would borrow more money than they could afford, and that it was a bank's responsibility, to itself, its shareholders, and its customers to hold the line and not let people borrow more than they could repay.

For whatever reasons, banks started moving the line, making it easy for people to borrow too much, which (as the banks predicted) they did. As everyone profited—for a while—only a few voices were hollering that the boom could not last.

Profit Maximization

The field of economics assumes that human beings are self-interested; as a result, they will naturally attempt to increase and even maximize their profits. This is a foundational element of capitalistic systems that is rooted in Adam Smith's classic, *The Wealth of Nations.* His oft-repeated quote presents the philosophy clearly: "It is not from the benevolence of the butcher, the brewer, or the baker that we expect our dinner, but from their regard to their own interest."

Twentieth-century economics shifted the focus from profit maximization to utility maximization; in other words, rational actors were now expected to maximize their utilities, which meant translating objective outcomes into an individual's own, subjective valuations. This makes eminent sense: after accumulating more and more chocolate, for instance, to the point where you cannot consume it pleasurably—even if you are a chocoholic—it probably pays to turn your attention to accumulating something else. (This also reflects the old notion of decreasing marginal returns: the more of something you have, the less valuable additional accumulation of that something becomes.)

There are several difficulties with the switch to utility maximization in terms of everyday life. First, money is extremely attractive: people try to get as much of it as they possibly can, seemingly without limit. If being a millionaire is good, being a billionaire is far, far better, and being a trillionaire is way, way better than that, at least in terms of the way people evaluate their lives. (Increasing wealth tends to have less impact on people's positive emotions.) Second, because people quickly acclimate to increasing wealth, they rarely experience the decreasing marginal value of additional money. Instead, as some people say, "money is money," which would not be the case if increasing amounts of cash were less valuable than initially acquired funds. Third, it is hard to calculate your own utilities, much less someone else's. For example, which would you rather have: an apple pie now or two in three weeks? Would you trade your car plus two bicycles for the same model car, one year newer? What about one that is only eight months newer?

Creating these questions is easy—answering them so that you can identify trades in which you are truly indifferent, which is a requirement of the utility approach—is extremely difficult, especially when your preferences may change from one day, one week, or one month to the next. Because you must have an intimate understanding of your indifference trade-offs to determine your exact utilities, it's not easy for most people to pin down their utility functions specifically.

This might be why it is easier to focus on the simple formula of maximizing profits. The corporate concept of maximizing shareholder returns reinforces this approach as well. This all feeds into business school education, which is dominated by an analytical, economic approach to problems. The result is a simple, loud, clarion call: maximize profits.

The Profit-Maximizing Organization

Let's imagine that you work for an organization that is led by a business school–educated MBA who has adopted a strong orientation toward maximizing the organization's profits. It is a publicly held company, so the shareholders support this approach, as it is in their best financial interests to do so. In fact, the CEO is clear and up front about the company's basic philosophy: it is all about maximizing shareholder value by being as profitable as it can be.

How does this company deal with you and your team members at salary time? How does it interact with reliable, loyal suppliers when a new firm offers to supply their material or personnel demands for a lower price? How does it respond to a long-term customer who has asked for a line of credit or for a refund when the company's products haven't performed up to expectations, even though it wasn't the company's fault? In many if not all of these situations, responding to short-term profit motives can hurt the company's long-term viability; it can also raise concerns about ethical behavior.

Let's contrast this approach with the idea of maximizing value rather than maximizing profits. (Note: This approach is similar to maximizing utilities, which is a value-oriented concept. The difference is that, unlike utilities, which are strictly individual in nature, the organization is attempting to maximize value that it can share with its various partners.)

If a company is trying to maximize value at salary time, it might realize that competent, trustworthy, dedicated employees are one of its most important assets: by respecting you and your team members and dealing with you transparently and consistently, rewarding your contributions and acknowledging them publicly, it creates value that might not have otherwise existed. Yes, this new value is amorphous: you can't take employee commitment to the bank. But that doesn't make it any less real. You and your team members' positive feelings toward the organization and their positive feelings toward you create a foundation of increased dependability, which can be critical for producing increased profits.

Similarly, when the company has had a positive history with a reliable supplier, continuing that relationship in the face of price pressures can also increase mutual value: you and your company become a better customer to that supplier, who may understandably reward you when their other customers must return to them because the new, low-cost supplier doesn't measure up to everyone's standards. You can also find yourself first in line when supplies are limited, allowing you to proceed with your business when your competitors can't.

Finally, who can beat dependable customers? They are not only valuable for their own sake; they are also valuable for their word-of-mouth advertising. Taking a short-term hit to preserve long-term gains and to promote goodwill creates additional value that you get to share.

In each case, creating value rather than seeking to maximize profits allows a company to produce *sustainable* profits for itself *and* for its partners. As a result, it becomes not just an ordinary partner, but an attractive partner—an organization that is good to work with because it tries to satisfy everyone's self-interest, not just its own. This can naturally lead to other employees, suppliers, and customers being attracted to the organization as well.

The same principles apply for great leaders: work to create value and you become an attractive partner. In this way you can build positive, profitable connections—with your team members, your customers, your superiors, and your suppliers. At the same time, it means that you can pursue your goals the right way, and never be accused of being either crass or unethical.

Values

The management literature is packed with articles that tell you to follow your values as a leader. This may be the literature's second most common topic, right after having a vision and communicating it well.

What the literature doesn't tell you is that, if you are not actively thinking about your values, you can easily make a quick decision or react to a critical situation in ways that don't match your values so well. This sets you up for after-the-fact regret.

How often do you have a quiet, calm day at work? For most leaders, the answer is a sharp laugh—"Never!" In the midst of the tumult and the hectic pace and the pressure to get more done in less time with fewer resources but still retain effectiveness, it's easy to get caught up in the daily maelstrom and not consider the value-oriented consequences of your actions.

If you are actually taking the time to read this book, however, you can also take some time to ask yourself a basic question: "Why do I do what I do?" You can add other questions, like "What is most important to me about my work?" or "What am I really trying to accomplish in life?" You are the only person who is in charge of achieving your personal goals. So obviously, it's up to you to know what they are and to do what you can to achieve them.

Yogi Berra was a great baseball player; he was also a very good manager. Over the years, however, his baseball skills have been overshadowed by the wisdom of many of his observations. His most famous quote is a beauty: "If you don't know where you're going, you might not get there."

If you are aware, really aware of your most important values, research tells us that it is much harder to violate them inadvertently. As a result it pays to think carefully about what is really important to you: if you can keep your values at the front of your mind, you can access them more easily so that you will be fully aware of what's critical when you face tough decisions.

A rare few people are incredibly aware of and committed to

their values. They choose all of their actions to be consistent with these central values. From a strictly personal point of view, they are both efficient and self-aware, and self-awareness is an indispensable characteristic for effective leaders. To paraphrase Yogi: if you don't know what you are good at and what you are bad at, how can you be successful as a leader?

Most of us are naturally influenced and sometimes even overwhelmed by our surroundings: we respond to time pressure by making quick decisions; we look at our immediate environment to determine what is appropriate; and when we are uncertain, we look to other people for guidance. In other words, our immediate contexts influence us profoundly and powerfully. When we are directly in tune with our core values, however, we are in command and we consider the pushes and pulls of outside forces—that is, other people and the situations we face—second. It is only then that we can take charge of our own lives and fulfill one of Ralph Waldo Emerson's famous maxims: "To be yourself in a world that is constantly trying to make you something else is the greatest accomplishment."

Sharing Your Values

Let's imagine that you have a clear sense of your own most important personal values. The obvious next question is, Should you share your values with your team members? If you do, you have done them a great service—you have given them information that can help them make better critical decisions by letting them know what you would want them to do even when you are not around.

The downside here is that, if you share your values with your team and you ever violate them, your integrity will be gone forever. Your team members depend on you and expect you to be consistent because it helps them make more consistent decisions as well as giving their actions more meaning. So you must be totally and completely committed to your values before you share them, especially when a situation seriously tests your resolve. Here's an example:

A few years ago I presented a workshop on negotiation and decision-making strategies to the members of one of the Australian divisions of the Young Presidents' Organization (YPO). (This is a wonderful organization of young executives who can turn to one another for guidance, for advice, and sometimes just for an ear. They are also completely committed to learning as much as they can about leadership.) Several of the participants traveled from Western Australia to attend our sessions in Sydney, and I had several conversations with one of them.

He was a remarkably conscientious, self-aware leader, and our conversations touched on a variety of topics during the three days of the workshop. At one point he mentioned that he only hired people who put their family before their jobs; he didn't want people in his organization if they put their jobs first. He felt strongly about this, saying that family-first people were the type of individuals he wanted to work with. He seemed both sincere and enlightened.

A year later I presented a similar workshop for another YPO group, this time in Macau. As it happened, my friend from Western Australia sent one of his vice presidents to the workshop. This was an opportunity for me to confirm what he had told me, so I asked the VP whether his boss really did live his values as he said he did. He told me the following story:

A few years before, the boss had hired a new executive. His first questions in the hiring process were about family and, as in all of his interviews, he made it clear that the organization's policy—his policy—was family first, work second. This fit the new recruit's own philosophy and, because the rest of the interview went well, he was hired.

Six months later, his wife was diagnosed with a malignant brain tumor. She battled the disease for eighteen months before passing away. Throughout that time, the new executive worked sparingly, as her treatment required almost all of his attention. This was the only part of his employment that was affected: he still received his full salary and all of his benefits. He returned to work, almost full-time, two weeks after his wife passed away, and he used his time at work as therapy to help him cope with his loss.

You can imagine what my storyteller said about his boss, the company, and the effect that this had on everyone in it. The boss was completely true to his values, even for a relatively new employee. He did not just share his values and he did not use them as a publicity tool, or for any other propaganda-oriented purpose. Instead, he came through in a tough situation: he *lived* his values, publicly, and everyone got the message.

Value and Values

These two words, *value* and *values*, are remarkably similar but, as we have seen, they are far from identical. By maximizing value, you become an attractive partner and put yourself in a position to be consistently profitable, not just financially but across many dimensions. Warren Buffett has often said that he looks to buy companies that are run like family businesses—in other words, organizations that try to create long-term profitability so they can pass it on to their descendants. Is there a better way to create a sustainable company than by being an attractive partner, one that everyone wants to do business with? Is there a better way for a leader to create long-term success than by being someone who works to create mutual value that everyone can share?

When we turn to values, it's critical for leaders to know their central values, to think about them and keep them at the front of their mind, and to *live* them. It makes life worthwhile and it helps a person to be a more predictable, consistent partner. Knowing your core values allows you to be consistent and careful: you will make better personal decisions and better organizational decisions if you know who you are and what you want to achieve.

Sharing your values can help you surround yourself with people who share those same values. This will help you create a supportive work environment that makes being a leader much, much easier. Whenever you read about the value and the values of diversity, realize that you don't want diversity in your team members' core values. Instead, it pays to hire people who are committed to and agree with your core values, and to seek diversity in all of their other dimensions.

Would the world economy still have suffered its meltdown if people had been maximizing value rather than profits? In its deepest sense, maximizing value is a pluralistic enterprise—it doesn't mean maximizing just one outcome. A philosophy of maximizing value might have pushed the financial markets of the world to consider more than the singular pursuit of profits. It's an idea that I hope we try in the future.

Tough decisions that are driven by a person's core values usually lead to long-term satisfaction, both with your actions and with who you are. Occasionally, the crushing consequences of following your values at the expense of your income can be overwhelming and pervasive. This is what makes these kinds of choices so difficult. There's not much benefit, for instance, in condemning people who bend their values to earn enough to pay the medical costs of a relative in need. This is a situation where one positive value conflicts with another. Resolving these kinds of issues thoughtfully would take at least another book, so we won't try to resolve them here. At the same time, when decisions like these arise, it's important to know what your most important values are—that way, good outcome or bad, you can press forward and not look back.

Unnatural Leaders

REAT LEADERS DO things differently. They stand out not just because they are so successful but because they don't act the way normal leaders act. This can sometimes make them seem eccentric; what it also means is that they don't let their natural tendencies interfere with being effective.

This chapter profiles seven idiosyncratic leaders. Each of them has been remarkably successful and each of them does things differently. In addition, they exemplify many of the lessons included in this book.

It is not a surprise that these great leaders share several common characteristics. First and foremost, they have all displayed intense passion for their work; they love what they do and it's my guess that their work doesn't feel like work to them at all. This also gives them added impetus to continue to be committed to what they are doing.

Second, they all have remarkable skill sets. They know their crafts; most of them apprenticed, albeit informally, before launching into their latest endeavors, but this is not true of all seven (as we will soon see).

Third, they all display tremendous determination. No one has ever had a career without obstacles; their ability to persevere in the face of adversity has helped put them in position to succeed. As one of them put it, "to be any good at it, you must concentrate so much that it becomes an obsession." They all seem a bit obsessive sometimes, in a good way.

And fourth, they have all done things differently. It's possible that their natural tendencies are not like the rest of ours. It's more likely, however, that they have learned to recognize when their natural tendencies might lead them astray, and they've put that learning into practice.

Their stories are both informative and inspirational. For the most part, they are not household names.* Obviously, the list could be much longer, as there are many amazing leaders throughout the world; these seven great leaders could easily be joined by your own personal favorites.

The list starts with a tremendously successful entrepreneur.

Michael Krasny

As we noted in the last chapter, in his late twenties, Michael Krasny recognized a business opportunity that combined his skills and his interests and he ran with it. He started and built CDW, literally from nothing to a hugely successful company. It has repeatedly been included in *Fortune*'s 100 Best Companies to Work For.

---

* This highly idiosyncratic list starts out with five men and finishes with two women. This ordering has nothing to do with gender—instead, it is the result of matching each of these great leader's central approaches with one of the main points from chapters 2 through 8. Thus, our first great leader is someone who Focuses on Them and our seventh De-emphasizes Profits.

Michael was also extremely talented at creating a positive, productive corporate culture. When I visited CDW's headquarters in the suburbs of Chicago, I saw signs all over the building that reminded people of Michael's approach to business, such as "It's only good if it's win/win," "Pay attention to your weaknesses. If you dwell on your successes, you will suffocate on your weaknesses," and "Hogs get slaughtered but pigs get fed."

Although culture is another of those amorphous but critical elements of an organization, we can see its impact in many ways. At CDW, the culture revealed itself in events like the company's support of a contingent of eighty employees traveling to New Orleans to assist the relief efforts following Hurricane Katrina, followed by a second contingent of three hundred more.

Michael's commitment to his philosophies also showed itself clearly when he decided to step down as CEO. He didn't step down when things were going badly. Sales of personal computers had fallen almost 23 percent in the last few months of 2000, compared with the last few months of 1999, but sales had not dropped at CDW: its net sales for 2000 had increased by 50 percent over its sales in 1999.

Instead, he simply felt that it was time for someone else to push the company forward. After announcing strong profits and the fact that sales had grown *for the twenty-seventh consecutive quarter,* right through the dot-com collapse (as if it had never existed), Michael released control of CDW to a newly hired CEO.

Most founder-CEOs don't take their companies as far as Michael did, and most of them don't have the wisdom to know when it's time to step down and let someone else take over. Another of Michael's philosophies may have had a hand in this decision: "Success means never being satisfied." He continued to want success for CDW and its people, even when he realized that he was no longer the one to drive it. In essence, he took *Do Nothing!* to whole new levels.

A more recent turning point for Michael and CDW was its sale to private equity investors in 2007. Michael was the company's largest stockholder, and he supported the sale. But he didn't walk away quietly. Instead, he sent a loud message to all of CDW's co-workers: they were going to share in the benefits of the sale and they would have a stake in CDW's future.

Here's what Michael did: when CEO John Edwardson sent an e-mail to all of CDW's employees announcing the completion of the sale, it included a message indicating that Michael had used more than 10 percent of his returns from the sale to set up a bonus and incentive plan based on each worker's current salary and their years of service. Those who were earning $40,000 and had been with the company for ten years, for example, learned that they would get a cash bonus of one third of their salary before the end of the year plus an additional two thirds of their salary in equity in the newly formed company. In other words, Michael created a huge fund of cash and equity to thank his coworkers for everything they had done for the company and to allow them to share in the new company's future.

This had an enormous effect on CDW's coworkers. As one of my executive students wrote, in two separate e-mails that day: "WOW. What a great leader!" and "You can't believe the energy at this place." John Edwardson also noted in his e-mail announcement that their legal and financial advisers, who had been involved in many similar corporate transactions, had never seen a founder contribute such a significant amount to a company's employees at the time of a sale.

These were leadership *actions* that had remarkably positive *reactions*. They also show how committed Michael was to his people. He is the epitome of a "Focus on Them" leader—someone who realized he could not do it on his own, that he depended on and needed loyal customers and loyal coworkers. He kept their interests at the forefront, even when he could have simply said "Thank you" and walked away.

Phil Jackson

Unlike most pro coaches, who pace up and down the floor, screaming orders at their players while they are trying to perform (what's up with that?), Phil Jackson sits down during games and actually lets his players play. In other words, he is an outstanding example of a successful leader who does nothing and who does things differently. How does he get away with it? Primarily because he helps his team to be prepared, *in advance*—that is, he facilitates their performance—then he leaves them alone so they can not only do their jobs but *know* they can do their jobs. Each season he also has a singular focus—to win the championship. All of these characteristics, and more, have contributed to his being the most successful coach in the history of professional basketball.

He had a rags-to-riches, storybook career (thirteen championships: eleven as a coach and two as a player). He grew up in rural Montana; his parents were both ministers, and there were some pretty strict rules in the Jackson household; for example, no television. He saw his first movie when he was a senior in high school and attended his first dance in college. He played basketball, football, and baseball, and ran track in high school. He was a scholarship basketball player for future NBA coach Bill Fitch at the University of North Dakota. In 1967, he was drafted by the New York Knicks. He was not a highly skilled offensive player, but he was a relentlessly energetic defender. He was the kind of person who obviously put everything he had into every game. As a result, he became a fan favorite and a favorite of his coach, Red Holzman. He made the starting lineup in 1974 and led the league in fouls—another indication that his energy exceeded his skills. His playing career ended in 1980.

In 1982, he got his first head coaching job, for the Albany Patroons in the Continental Basketball Association (essentially the NBA's minor league). In 1984 he also started coaching in the summer league in Puerto Rico. In 1987, he made it to the NBA as an assistant coach for the Chicago Bulls; he was promoted to head coach two years later.

Phil Jackson was not an ordinary basketball coach. Among many idiosyncrasies, he was well known for giving each of his players a carefully selected book at the start of each season's longest road trip. (Not all of his players read these books, but they appreciated the thought that went into their particular selection.) He mixed Zen Buddhism and Native American culture into his coaching style, even to the point of decorating the Bulls' meeting room with Native American artifacts, as if it were their own private teepee.

When great basketball coaches write books, they often use chapter titles that are directive, explanatory, or descriptive, such as "Learn to Be a Great Communicator," "Building Confidence," or "Complacency." They all focus on how to play the game.

Phil Jackson's books are different. A quick look at *Sacred Hoops: Spiritual Lessons of a Hardwood Warrior,* which describes his early career and the first three Bulls' championships, reveals some directive chapter titles like "Aggressiveness Without Anger" and "Selflessness in Action" and "Being Aware Is More Important Than Being Smart." But it also includes other chapters like "If You Meet Buddha in the Lane, Feed Him the Ball," "Experiments in the Cockroach Basketball League," and "You Can't Step in the Same River Twice." There are also section titles within the chapters such as "Zen Bones," "Intimacy with All Things," "Fish Don't Fly," and "The Howl of the Ego." In other words, his books are different, too.

In essence, he approaches coaching by trying to engage his players' minds as well as their bodies; he even tries to engage their souls. Basketball is a tremendously demanding, physical sport, as the players must excel at a series of inconsistent tasks: they must run fast, jump high, and shoot softly. By pushing them *indirectly*, Jackson got them to think and to feel, increasing their engagement in the here-and-now and embedding his ideas more deeply within them. He had a truly amazing, magical approach to leadership, especially when you realize that his team members were more than occasionally afflicted by incredibly large egos.

Here's an example of how his indirect approach to leadership works in a completely different context. Our daughter Kate is a remarkable, wonderful person; just because I'm her father, it doesn't mean that I'm biased (much). One of her many great qualities is that she is incredibly tenacious; in particular, when she was young and she decided that she wanted to do something, it was almost impossible to stop her, even if her goal was not particularly wise. We soon learned that, even though it seemed like the only solution, screaming "STOP!" was not very effective, as it only revealed one more obstacle (us) to her ultimate goal.

She was about seven years old when we discovered a much better solution. During one of many calm interludes, we asked her to pretend there was a button located right in the middle of her collarbone, just below her throat. This was going to be her "Stop Button." Rather than raising our voices and hollering "Stop!" when she got revved up and was headed for disaster, we asked her, calmly and in a normal voice, to "Press your button." We pressed the same spot on our collarbones at the same time.

It worked for years. In fact, it worked long enough that, by the time she was a teenager, she had learned how to get herself under control with very little input from us.

Why did it work so well? For at least two important reasons. First, we were no longer screaming at her—which had been completely counterproductive, as it only led to her increasing her resistance to us and her commitment to her goal. Second, she was directly involved: *she* was the one pressing the button; *she* was the person who was in control. By becoming responsible for controlling herself, she was able to channel her tremendous energy in more appropriate directions. This is just what coaches and leaders hope for.

More conventionally, as chapter 3 notes, Phil Jackson was remarkably successful at determining the roles that each of his players needed to fulfill for the team to be successful. He made sure they knew the deep nature of their role, its importance, and its limits. This helped the players on the Bulls and Lakers championship teams to take advantage of their skills in a way that meshed their collective roles into a truly effective, complementary, and cohesive team.

Jackson was blessed with extraordinary players, including Michael Jordan, Scottie Pippen, Kobe Bryant, and Shaquille O'Neal—all of them simply remarkable athletes—but they have won all of their championship rings (except one)* with Phil Jackson as their coach. It is not just supremely talented superstars that have led to his success; he also had to work effectively with his superstars *and* his other players to mold an effective team.

Add to this the fact that he has taken on some particularly problematic but talented players (for example, Dennis Rodman and Ron Artest) and still succeeded, and it is a testament to his ability to help all of his players fulfill their roles within a system that gave them the potential to win big and win consistently.

Last but not least, another of the many reasons why Phil Jackson was so successful as a leader was that (as noted) each year he

---

* Shaquille O'Neal won a championship playing with the Miami Heat in 2006. This was the only time that any of these four players won a championship without Phil Jackson as their coach. In fact they played for more seasons (33), collectively, with other coaches than they did with Phil (32), but they won a total of 20 championship rings on his teams.

had a singular goal—to win the championship—and all of his efforts were directed toward achieving it. When he coached older players, even brilliant older players, he made sure they were rested and ready at playoff time, rather than being burned out by the grind of the regular season.

It is also why, during the season, even when the team was struggling, he called time-outs only rarely: this allowed his players to discover what they needed to do to get back on track. By letting them overcome their momentary struggles *on their own*, he made sure they were prepared to overcome these same kinds of struggles when it mattered even more, in the playoffs. His teams were exceedingly successful because his players knew how to act as their own leaders, on the floor, during a game.

Phil Jackson is a perfect example of a leader who started at the end, prior to each season, and worked his way back to the start of his preparations, laying out each step to achieve his ultimate goal. All along the way, with a book for the road trip and a nod to Zen Buddhism and the holistic approach of Native American philosophy, he constructed a nonlinear path for himself and his team, one that increased their chances of holding another trophy at the end of the season. No one has ever done it better.

Soichiro Honda

Soichiro Honda started his career as a mechanic. Ultimately, he became the founder and chairman of the Honda Motor Company. They still talk about him within the company, even though he passed away more than twenty years ago.

He knew engines, inside and out, technically and intuitively. He was a gifted, charismatic leader; he was also a creative genius who had three or four new ideas almost every single day. At the same time, he invited and embraced people who criticized his ideas: he knew that this would save him from overreaching. In addition, he surrounded himself with talented people whose skill sets differed from and complemented his own: this helped him build a stellar, diverse organization.

Honda grew up in a small village outside of Tokyo. His parents both worked with their hands—his mother was a weaver and his father was a blacksmith who also repaired bicycles and even did a little dental work. The kids at his school called him the "black-nosed weasel" because he was always poking around his father's forge.

He was always ingenious. As a kid, he got into trouble when he used the rubber from a bicycle pedal to make a copy of his family's seal so that he could approve his own grade reports without his parents' ever seeing them. He got caught when he expanded his enterprise, making stamps for his friends without recognizing that, unlike the symmetric characters in his own name, his friends needed mirror images of their names for the stamps to come out correctly.

Honda was fascinated with engines. At fifteen, he left home to apprentice with a car mechanic. Because he was so young, the owner had him care for his child, so Honda carted the baby around the shop with him, watching the mechanics work. He opened his own shop at the age of twenty-two. He demanded quality workmanship and was known to throw tools when his employees' efforts were not up to his standards.

In his late twenties, he focused on producing better piston rings for small engines. He was a mechanic rather than a leader, working day and night, sometimes sleeping in his workshop; he even pawned his wife's jewelry when he was short of funds. Like any budding entrepreneur, he was not yet in *Do Nothing!* mode; instead, he was the driving force—in action, vision, and execution. It also helped that he was doggedly persistent: after some humiliating failures, he finally perfected his design and ultimately sold the business to Toyota. Perseverance paid.

He was interested in motorcycles and was a successful racer himself. (He tried his hand as a professional race-car driver, too, until a crash almost killed him.) After the war, the new Honda Motor Company's first product was a small engine that could be attached to a bicycle; they called it a *batabata* after the sound the engine made. Its success led to the production of their first, small motorcycle, which they (fittingly) called the Dream. Within a decade Honda became the world's leading motorcycle manufacturer.

When they started the company, Honda was in charge of engineering and his friend Takeo Fujisawa handled the business side. More than once they came close to bankruptcy, but they continued to innovate and expand, from small motorcycles to small automobiles, even in the face of serious government resistance to the introduction of a new automobile manufacturer.

Their move into automobiles had early roots: when Honda was a kid and saw a car for the first time, "I could not understand how it could move under its own power. And when it had driven past me, without even thinking why, I found myself chasing it down the road, as hard as I could run." We see this same kind of passion and fascination in almost all outstanding leaders.

Honda's venture into automobiles, especially in the United States, received a huge boost when the Environmental Protection Agency reacted to the 1970s gas shortage with new regulations that forced Honda's competitors to add antipollution devices to their vehicles. Honda's tiny CVCC engine already met the new requirements and needed no modifications. Honda's expertise in making small, attractive cars put the Honda Motor Company in perfect position for another wave of success.

Like so many unnatural leaders, Honda did things differently. Unlike other Japanese businessmen, for instance, he enjoyed talking with the press; he was not a suit-and-tie executive, but dressed casually; he was outspoken in his admiration of American business and Western lifestyles; and he promoted people on the basis of their performance rather than their age: "Each individual should work for himself. People will not sacrifice themselves for the company. They come to work at the company to enjoy themselves."

He also combined his creativity and his tenacious determination with an openness that helped him weed out his own bad ideas. He and Fujisawa would start each workday by sharing a pot of tea. Honda would describe his newest ideas and Fujisawa would ask him questions about them: "How will this market respond?" or "How will that division react?" Almost every day, by the time they had finished their tea, they had thrown out all of Honda's ideas.

There are two morals to this story. First, although it's great to have creative people in your company, most of their ideas are lousy. (This is how the creative process works.) It's critical to find a way to eliminate the bad ideas, gently. Second, it pays to be open to criticism. Honda invited and embraced Fujisawa's questions; he wanted to know when his ideas wouldn't work. This reverses our natural tendencies: when most people have a new idea, they hope that it garners praise and they are disappointed when it is criticized. Honda took the opposite approach, pushing to discover when his ideas would not work so he could avoid a narrowly supported idea that might have been doomed to failure. In other words, he valued ideas over his own ego—a great combination for a leader.

He also expanded his ideas-first, me-second approach into his hiring philosophy: "If you hire only those people you understand, the company will never get people better than you are. Always remember that you often find outstanding people among those you don't particularly like." He was not only willing to trust Fujisawa completely; he even hired and trusted people he didn't like.

Honda retired in 1973 but, rather than foll[...] tional Japanese route of fading into the backgrou[...] ary chairman, he became the company's "supre[...] spent eighteen months visiting seven hundred of [...] production plants and dealerships, sending a ser[...] observations and recommendations back to corpor[...] ters. He had a great time during this journey, and he continued to be driven by his broad, philosophical outlook: "The value of life can be measured by how many times your soul has been deeply stirred."

As Clint Eastwood said in one of his Dirty Harry movies, "A man's got to recognize his limitations." Honda was brilliant in so many ways but he was not a great organizer. Because he recognized this, and because he completely trusted his friend and colleague Takeo Fujisawa, he could focus all of his attention, literally, on the engines in his businesses: he knew that Fujisawa would take care of everything else. He frequently noted that "Without Fujisawa, we would have gone bust a long time ago." In turn, Fujisawa responded by saying, "Without Honda, we would have never become this big."

They were two close friends who took advantage of their different but complementary skills. Their bond of trust allowed them to work together seamlessly. Not only that, the office at the top of the Honda Motor Company was psychologically safe, and this safe, trusting atmosphere permeated the organization. It would not have worked so well any other way.

Norbert Brainin

Norbert Brainin was the first violinist of the Amadeus String Quartet, one of the twentieth century's most renowned ensembles. They initially called themselves the Brainin Quartet; after a hey changed their name and continued playing together, without any change in the quartet's membership, for forty years.

I was fortunate enough to interview each of them seven years before they ended their run, when Peter Schidlof, the viola player, passed away. Norbert Brainin was the heart and soul of the group; for him playing quartet music was akin to religion. His passionate commitment both to the music and to his team members is a model for first violinists and leaders of all kinds.

He was born in 1923 in Vienna. His parents were not musicians but they loved music, and when Norbert was six, they went to Yehudi Menuhin's Viennese debut. This inspirational experience led to his seventh birthday present, a quarter-sized violin, which seemed to seal his destiny: "I picked up a fiddle and I never put it down. . . . I wanted to be a violinist. I knew then and there. I actually knew. It's an amazing thing."

Because of his Jewish heritage, and after the death of both of his parents, he left Eastern Europe and immigrated to London in 1938. During the war, England established a series of internment camps to keep track of "enemy aliens." Brainin was housed in Shropshire, where he met Peter Schidlof; they played together and soon became fast friends. Schidlof, in turn, met Siegmund Nissel, who became the quartet's second violinist.

The war was still on when Brainin left the internment camp, so he took a job as a machine tool fitter—not the best work for a violinist's sensitive hands. He also performed whenever he could: "When I came to London, I played a lot of chamber music with amateurs, which was very good for me. Some of them paid me."

After Schidlof and Nissel's release from the internment camp, they all studied with the same teacher, Max Rostal, who connected them with Martin Lovett, who soon became the quartet's cellist.

After the war, in 1946, Brainin won a major competition; his playing of the Beethoven Violin Concerto with the London

Philharmonic at the Royal Albert Hall led a reviewer to write: "Norbert is dynamic—he electrified everyone. . . . extraordinary playing—intense, burning, but very controlled . . . he does everything with the whole of himself—eating, playing and laughing."

That same year the quartet held its debut concert at Wigmore Hall; it was also a major event, leading to a line of people stretching around the block. This opened all sorts of doors, including the chance to play in Germany, which they only agreed to after lengthy discussion.

Their early rehearsals were chaotic contests, as their goal was to discover and reproduce the ideal interpretation of the music that they loved so much. As Brainin put it, "For a group to whom this is a life's work, everything that happens within the quartet is life and death. . . . You have to argue." Brainin was an avid student of classical music and its history, so he was remarkably well prepared to push his interpretation of a piece. He felt that the composer's intentions were the sole basis for a "true" interpretation. His intense dedication to seeking this truth meant that he could argue incessantly. But the truth that he and his colleagues sought actually changed from one performance to the next, albeit subtly: "You play in time with each other and, within the framework of this 'playing in time,' your playing becomes free. Every now and then, you may lengthen something a bit but that must be balanced out somehow, by taking away from somewhere else. . . . It must be 'both free and rigorous.' "

He always knew what he wanted to hear. His persistence in achieving that made him hard to work with but remarkably successful. Yet he also knew that, ultimately, all four of them had to agree: "Everyone must be satisfied with what they are doing. You don't have majority decisions. A minority of one can break up the whole thing. If he doesn't like it, he can just go. You must satisfy everybody and you can only do that by talking." He also realized that this kind of collective agreement, once achieved, made them more effective and more cohesive: "If you have a problem and you get together and solve it, that makes you much stronger. You have solved it and you have proved your ability to solve it . . . and the less likely you break up."

He trusted, respected, and liked his fellow quartet members, and he loved playing Beethoven: "It is worth a lifetime of hard work, study, practice, concertizing, this and that, to learn how to play the quartets of Beethoven. If you have done that, it is worth having been alive. It is a true mirror of your life, of the spirit, of our civilization. . . . The late quartets are pure spirit. They are the continuation of the Old and New Testament put to music. He's like a prophet. . . . I don't know why I'm telling you all this. I don't want to say it . . . in cold blood. I want people to hear it, when I play it, when it comes out of me."

Brainin was a voluble, fun-loving, absentminded, excitable person; he was a brilliant, instinctive, sometimes impetuous musician. Playing the lead in the late Beethoven quartets was an awesome technical challenge, one that young violinists typically avoided. Brainin, in contrast, seemed to play it effortlessly.

During my interview with him, it was clear that he completely understood the conundrums that teams and their leaders all face. In his case, each of the members of a quartet needed the skills of a soloist, but they also had to have the ability and the motivation to play together. Any of them could play for a large orchestra and earn far more than they did in a quartet, but they all wanted to have a say in how they played the music they loved. At the same time, however, the music was designed for the first violinist to be the leader: it comes across best when the leader is in control. Within the quartet (and many other teams), there is an inherent clash between the democratic influence that everyone desires and a leader's need to retain control.

Brainin knew all of this, almost instinctively. As he put it, "I shaped and molded this quartet. I make them play the way I want them to play. I don't tell them 'you have to play like this'—that's impossible. I have to lead by example. I have to make them realize that what I'm doing is good." At the same time, he said, "You don't lay down the law—you argue. You put forward your point strongly and incisively and persuasively with complete honesty. *And* you must be prepared to be persuaded by a superior argument. . . . You have to be completely open-minded, but at the same time, you must *not* compromise!" He also couldn't help adding, "Yes, I'm probably more persuasive than the others."

He was not shy about his role in the group: "I was always the one who had the ideas. . . . I was the *moving* spirit of the whole thing. . . . I am the first violin. I am *primus inter pares* (the first among equals)." But "False authority is when you pick up an axe. Real authority is when you sit *down*. And this is my authority. . . . I have to inspire them with my play."

Norbert Brainin understood the competing dualities that were required of a leader: he had to release control and retain it, simultaneously and even a bit deviously. He did it with intense passion, remarkable technical ability, and a warm smile on his face. This made him the most important element in the Amadeus Quartet's remarkable success and their amazing artistic achievements.

Michael Abrashoff

Unnatural leader number five is Michael Abrashoff, an ex–Navy captain, leadership consultant, and author (whom we have already cited in chapters 2 and 6). He admits to never having met a public address system that he didn't like. He took over the worst-performing ship in the Navy and turned it into its best-performing ship. In the process, he instituted changes that the entire Navy adopted. As the captain of the USS *Benfold,* he was remarkably effective at delegating authority and helping people feel good about what they do.

Abrashoff is a native of Altoona, Pennsylvania; he graduated from the U.S. Naval Academy in 1982 and, after a series of interesting assignments, became the military assistant to William J. Perry, the secretary of defense. This allowed him to travel the world on missions of national security.

He was thirty-six when he took over the *Benfold*, the youngest commanding officer in the Pacific Fleet. The *Benfold* is a guided missile destroyer and, at its deployment in 1996, it was a $1 billion technological marvel. It could fight warplanes, missiles, other ships, submarines, or attack shore targets; it had its own missiles, antisubmarine torpedoes, and space for landing Seahawk helicopters. It was an amazing ship.

When Abrashoff took over, it was also afflicted with exceptionally low morale, high turnover, and poor performance. Abrashoff used an approach he called GrassRoots Leadership, replacing command and control with commitment and cohesion. During his stewardship, promotions tripled; operating expenses fell by 25 percent; and the *Benfold* won the Spokane Trophy for being the best ship in the Pacific Fleet. Abrashoff and his crew also reduced turnover from 72 percent to an unprecedented 1 percent.

Reenlistments are critical for the Navy, as already-trained sailors can do much more than new recruits can. In fact, reenlistments are such a big deal that sailors can select almost any naval officer they want to conduct their reenlistment ceremony. As it happens, an ex–Navy officer who attended one of my classes conducted a reenlistment ceremony for a young sailor on the *Benfold* and he told me about the experience. When the sailor selected him, he said that he hoped to introduce him to Captain Abrashoff, but he feared that Abrashoff would not have much time, as he was so busy running the ship.

When he arrived at the *Benfold*, Abrashoff met him on the dock and escorted him aboard. Not only that, he spent the entire day with him, showing him around. Every time they encountered a sailor, Abrashoff introduced him and asked each of his sailors to tell their visitor about their duties. All day long, Abrashoff gave his sailors a chance to show off what they could do and be publicly acknowledged for their contributions.

Although this was a relaxed, easy day, it was completely clear that the process left every sailor beaming with pride. And what had Abrashoff done? Absolutely nothing.

Is there a better way to motivate people? Throughout *It's Your Ship*, Abrashoff's fine book on leadership, he presents a series of similar stories of everyday events that demonstrate how effective a leader can be. He did not hesitate to push his people to excel, but he did it respectfully and supportively. The result was a group of more than three hundred sailors who were both productive and proud.

Maggie Doyne

Maggie Doyne is the founder, builder, and director of Kopila Valley Children's Home for orphans, the founder and principal of the Kopila Valley Primary School, and the founder and director of the BlinkNow Foundation, all in Nepal. Although she may not think about things this way, she has taken a strict, economic utility analysis to the limit by ignoring her own personal needs and, instead, working with people whose utility is low so that her actions can have maximum impact. She typifies a leader who has identified a need in others that she can help to fulfill, and she is a consummate orchestrator.

Maggie grew up in Mendham, New Jersey. Her mother is a

nurse practitioner and her father is a stay-at-home dad. She was an outstanding student in high school, earning top grades and participating in three sports. Rather than going to college right after high school, though, Maggie decided to travel the world.

She was doing volunteer work with children in a poor area of India when she met a Nepalese girl who had been driven out by their civil war. After the border reopened, they traveled together for forty-eight hours on a public bus plus three days walking to reach the girl's home. Along the way, Maggie saw kids using hammers to break rocks that they could then sell as gravel.

She met "hundreds of orphan children. I fell in love with their bright eyes and beautiful smiles, but was shocked to see them barely surviving without the most basic things that I had grown up with as a child." One of those kids was a little girl named Hema, a rock breaker and scavenger who did not attend school but always greeted Maggie with a warm hello.

Hema was a turning point for Maggie, who decided to pay for Hema's schooling: "I knew I couldn't do anything about a million orphans, but what if I started with this girl?" The school fees were seven dollars; Hema's uniform was eight dollars. "It became addictive," she said. "I said, if I can help one girl, why not five? Why not ten?"

Her growing aspirations were a tremendous spur: Maggie found a phone, called her parents, and asked them to wire her all of her savings—$5,000. Obviously, this request prompted more than a few concerns on the home front, but Maggie's parents knew there was no stopping her once she had decided on a course of action. Maggie used the money to buy land and then began working with people in the village to build her orphans' home. "I met children in need of a home and decided to build one for them. I wanted it to be the kind of home and the kind of childhood that I thought every child in the world deserved. It was really as simple as that."

On a trip home to New Jersey she raised an additional $25,000, and her orphans' home became a reality. With a constantly increasing number of needy orphans, there is always the hope of further expansion. Winning a $20,000 prize funded by Maybelline was a major boost. Winning $100,000 more in another contest provided the funds for the construction of her school.

With each new endeavor, Maggie faced new challenges. At the school, she repeatedly bucked tradition, only hiring teachers who pledged that they would not use corporal punishment and hiring low-caste mothers to prepare the kids' food. The school includes vocational skills as a central element in the curriculum, teaching the kids how to raise livestock and repair bicycles so they will have skills they can use to support themselves. Both boys *and* girls are enrolled—a big plus for the community, as girls' education is related to lower birth rates.

People in the area have given her tremendous support; she, in turn, created a Nepali board of directors made up entirely of people from Surkhet, the local village. As she notes, "The women on the Nepali Board are mothers, shopkeepers, and community leaders; they cannot read; they cannot write; none of them have been afforded even an elementary school education; but they are among the wisest, brightest, most amazing women I have ever had the privilege of working beside. I learn from them every day."

The Kopila Valley Children's Home currently houses 40 orphans; Maggie is their legal guardian. The Kopila Valley Primary School enrolls more than 250 kids, many of whom are the first of their families to attend school. The school provides an education as well as health care and a daily nutritious meal; it is run by 23 Nepali faculty and staff who hope to expand.

All of these ventures have put Maggie's personal life on hold. Someday she might be able to pursue a romance or go to college. At the moment, however, she has devoted herself to the poor people of Surkhet, eight thousand miles away from her home.

She believes that when children have their most basic needs and rights fulfilled—a safe home, medical care, an education, and love—they can grow to be leaders and end cycles of poverty and violence. Her BlinkNow Foundation's philosophy: "in the blink of an eye, we can all make a difference."

She maintains an active blog that keeps people informed about the kids' day-to-day lives. Her comments and observations on everything that is happening in Kopila Valley provide a spur for others to help her do more than she ever could on her own. In essence, she has leveraged her own "anything is possible" philosophy to attract people from the surrounding community, from her original home in New Jersey, and from around the world. She is the symbolic center of an amazing enterprise. And, although she is willing to roll up her sleeves and pitch in, she has had her greatest impact by connecting with people who can't help but respond and support her ventures.

Along the way, she has established important performance goals for herself: every day she strives to focus on "making sure that my children feel safe and loved." She may be having an impact on only one small corner of the globe, but "the peace in our home and the joy of our children often radiates to our neighbors and our village, the city we live in and people who come to visit from other countries in the world." As she puts it, "What if my dream was to walk across this dry river bed one day and not see a single child breaking stone? That's what I want. I want to create a world that I want to see every day and I think that we have the power to do that."

More than anything else, she has focused her attention, her energy, and her skills on advancing learning, which can never be removed from the children she has touched, and which they can share to help support even more of the people who need it. Margaret Mead, the famous anthropologist, once said, "Never doubt that a small group of thoughtful, committed citizens can change the world. Indeed, it is the only thing that ever has." She could have said "one person" instead of a small group, and she could have been thinking of Maggie Doyne.

When the problems of the world seem overwhelming, Maggie stops so that she can "try to focus on the smaller things that I know are in my control: bathing my children, trimming their fingernails, cooking a meal together, and reading a bedtime story. Then my heart feels peaceful again and then I can keep going."

Ralph Waldo Emerson once said, "To laugh often and much; to win the respect of intelligent people and the affection of children; to earn the appreciation of honest critics and to endure the betrayal of false friends. To appreciate beauty; to find the best in others; to leave the world a bit better whether by a healthy child, a garden patch, or a redeemed social condition; to know that even one life has breathed easier because you have lived. This is to have succeeded." Maggie Doyne knows this already, and she is only twenty-four years old.

Oprah Winfrey

Oprah Winfrey is a media and entertainment superstar. She is the richest self-made woman in America; by some reports, she is also the highest-earning woman in America. Several media sources have called her the most influential woman in the world. Her TV show reached millions of viewers each day; it allowed her to display her leadership philosophy openly and clearly, for all to see and admire.

She wasn't always a star. She was born out of wedlock to a teenage mom in Mississippi. She lived at various times with her grandmother, her mother, and her father in Mississippi, Milwaukee, and Nashville. She did not grow up with her two half-sisters or her half-brother, and two of the three have passed away, due to drug- and AIDS-related causes. She ran away from home when she was thirteen and was pregnant at fourteen. Her son died shortly after he was born.

She was popular and an honors student in high school, and her skills on the school speech team led to a scholarship to Tennessee State University. She won the Miss Black Tennessee beauty pageant and worked as a part-time newscaster on a local radio station. She moved up to being the news anchor at WLAC-TV in Nashville and at WJZ-TV in Baltimore by the time she was twenty-two. When she was twenty-four, she became the cohost of a local talk show.

Her star rose dramatically in 1984 when she moved to Chicago and took over WLS-TV's morning talk show. *The Oprah Winfrey Show* soon became the number-one talk show on TV. Her star continues to grow with a media empire in print, film, production, and television. She has also built a Leadership Academy for Girls in South Africa, and she has been a visiting professor at Northwestern University's Kellogg School of Management (my school), teaching a sold-out course on leadership. She began her own TV network, OWN, in January 2011, giving her legions of fans access to Oprah (or at least Oprah-related broadcasts) 24/7.

She is driven by an unflinching personal philosophy: she believes in self-awareness and the need to be true to yourself. She is the epitome of a values-driven leader. Her mantra is "lead your best life" and she inspires people to believe it.

It is no surprise that her approach to life comes across as sincerely religious. In an interview in *U.S. News & World Report* in 2005, she spoke of her responsibilities as a calling: "We live in a society that doesn't pay attention to you unless you have money or fame. . . . The responsibility of people who have money and fame and some kind of clout is to use that in a meaningful way."

She runs her many businesses "more from the heart, gut, instinct, which are all the same." She is intensely attuned to her own inner voice: "What I've learned is that when I don't know what to do, do nothing. Sit still and listen for that small voice that will always lead you and guide you. If you're quiet and listen, you will hear it."

She also lets people know that she truly cares about them. She told her TV audience: "I want you all to know that my relationship with you is one that I hold very dear. Your trust in me, the sharing of your precious time every day with me has brought me the greatest joy I have ever known."

Her personal leadership course at Kellogg constantly focused on two main targets: intentions and being authentic. She pushed her students to look inward to know what they truly valued and what they really wanted to do, to admit their mistakes and recognize their weaknesses. "I haven't planned one thing—ever. I have just been led by a strong instinct, and I have made choices based on what was right for me at the time."

She treats her employees very well: Harpo Inc. houses a café, a workout facility, and a spa. A job at Harpo starts with four weeks' vacation; some people have as many as eleven. "I don't yell at people. I don't mistreat people. I don't talk down to people, so no one else in this building, in this vicinity, has the right to do it. Treating people with respect is the most important thing to me. It's not just talk." To celebrate the show's twenty years on national TV, she took her staff and their families—more than a thousand people—to Hawaii for a vacation.

It may be hard to think of Oprah Winfrey as a *Do Nothing!* leader because she is so actively involved in so many different activities. (I can't help thinking that she might benefit by doing less!) When she taught at Kellogg, for instance, some of my PhD students were her graders: they read all of her students' assignments and commented on them for her. But Oprah didn't allow them to write their comments directly on the students' papers. Instead, she had them put their comments on Post-it notes and attach them in the appropriate places on each student's paper.

Why? Because she read every paper herself and added even more comments. Although this was great for her students, was it the best use of her time? Maybe not, particularly since doing less grading might have extended her teaching career: it is no surprise that her publicly stated reason for stopping was the onus of grading.

Oprah is not a classic *Do Nothing!* leader (yet), because she still acts as if she is in building mode, much like a new entrepreneur. Like our other unnatural leaders, she lives her values and she is particularly notable for espousing them so openly. Her leadership style is based on a single, central value—her intense love for people. She loves her audience. She loves her employees. She loves her friends and her business partners. They all know it and they know they can count on it. The results speak for themselves, and are a testament to her talents, her ambitions, and the relentless pursuit of her vision.

Seven Unnatural Leaders

In one way or another, as well as by necessity, all of these seven leaders are *Do Nothing!* leaders: they could not have accomplished so much on their own. In addition, although we might think of them as being a particular "type" of *Do Nothing!* leader, they are all multifaceted, complex people with a variety of leadership skills. In fact, each of them has many, most, or all of the characteristics that we've outlined throughout this book.* Although we might think of Michael Krasny as a "Focus on Them" leader or Phil Jackson as a "Start at the End" leader, they are much more than that. Here's why:

Michael Krasny has the perfect focus for someone in sales: he

* In this section we highlight many of *Do Nothing!*'s central ideas in bold type.

tries to discover what people need and then provide it to them. His approach with his coworkers fit this mind-set as well: he used **structural control** to keep them positive about their work and their mission while they focused on the jobs they needed to do—even when he was not around. More generally, he put other people's concerns at the forefront of his thoughts and actions; he only put himself in the center of the picture in the early days of the company, when he made great use of **comparative advantage** by combining his skills at sales with his fascination with computers. Along the way he pushed himself and everyone else to do better, as his "Philosophies of Success" are all about doing more—for example, "Good luck many times comes disguised as hard work."

Phil Jackson's **overarching goal** of winning an NBA championship, each and every season, was the driving force behind all of his strategies: he started at the end, à la **backwards induction**, and constructed each season's strategies to achieve that ultimate goal. In the process, he **pushed**, cajoled, **rewarded**, and **sincerely cared** for his players, all to engage their minds and their souls as well as their bodies. At the same time, he **resisted the urge to take control**, more than any other coach I have ever seen. His expansive strategy was dynamic, broad, cyclical, and personally inclusive—**facilitation and orchestration** at its best.

Soichiro Honda had a right-hand man, Takeo Fujisawa, throughout his career. Like many great leaders, Honda was the front man, the one with the ideas and the far-ranging strategic vision, and Fujisawa was his second violinist. Honda not only **trusted him more** than we might expect: their mutual trust was unassailable. Honda was a demanding leader who did not push too hard, as the inherent nature of the tasks of constructing a new motorcycle or a new car required a focus on **incremental progress rather than quantum leaps** in mechanical innovation. Add to this his immense creativity and his **intense drive to** learn—in other words, **a strong growth mind-set**—and we see a leader who was a constantly moving, unstoppable force, pulling everyone else along.

Norbert Brainin was a superb musician: he was a brilliant soloist who also saw all of the paradoxes of leading a team by creating **a democratic atmosphere** while he still **retained control**. He was a true wire walker: he was open to his team members' convincing him when they were right, but he was the one who played the tune. They knew that he was leading them but they felt that **they owned the quartet**, too, as **they each had critical roles**. He was relentless in his pursuit of achieving the truth in the music that he and his quartet members loved so much: he **knew his goals** and pushed to achieve them, tenaciously. At the same time, he **knew what his team members could do** and he **helped everyone** in the quartet **know one another's skills**. He also focused on **doing things the right way** to move them to peak performances, **knowing that good outcomes would follow great execution**. He was unique among our other natural leaders because you could hear the beautiful music he and his team played—literally.

Michael Abrashoff was a constant presence on his ship, **walking the deck** or using the public address system. Unlike other notable leaders, he had a built-in opportunity to **get on the balcony** because his ship had a bridge that allowed him to look out over everyone's activities. He allowed and **encouraged each of his sailors to show off their skills**, and he **recognized them**, immediately and publicly, when they did. His *Do Nothing!* approach gave his people the power to act, to control their own destinies, and to contribute to a greater good. He **instilled pride in them even as he pushed them to excel** and, because he is such a good storyteller, he got his points across indirectly, and effectively. He was the epitome of a leader who exhibited **tough love**: his sailors knew that he **truly cared** about them and that he was all about **pushing** them to do their jobs as well as they possibly could.

Maggie Doyne carved out a corner of the world and turned a fairly hopeless situation into a thriving community. She has grown into adulthood helping other people thrive and learn. I'm not sure she realizes how powerfully **her actions influence other people's reactions**: it's hard not to rally around her when you see her **unflagging commitment to her goals**. In addition, her great **empathy** for the people of Nepal allows her to have a clear vision that drives her and her support teams as they help children get the normal things that every kid needs. In the process, they collectively **create long-lasting, sustainable value**. Although she has not enjoyed the easy life that many of us experience in modern-day America, check out her blog—what you will come away with is utter joy.

Oprah Winfrey listens to her own inner voice, which continues to tell her the right path to follow, as it always has. She **knows her values and lives them** religiously, even as she engages a huge following of supporters whom she **trusts more** and more, thereby **diversifying her interpersonal risks**. She is **not blinded by fear** but inspired by the possibilities she sees. Ironically, I think of her as a person who **de-emphasizes profits**, even though she is incredibly rich! As a result, she shows how attention to doing things right ultimately results in great outcomes.

All seven of these people are outstanding, unnatural leaders. They are smart, talented, and passionate. They do their homework, they have high standards and **high expectations**, and they **get into their team members' shoes**. They **ask lots and lots of questions** and **they listen** to the answers that they get. They know what they are after, they constantly push themselves to get better, and **they create tremendous value**. They believe in the power of people, **they delegate** like crazy, they treat people with respect as they push them to do more, and they attract people, even as they sometimes seem eccentric or counternormative.

Their stories are an inspiration, a model, and a guide to

effective leadership. They show us all how easy it can be. Not that there are no bumps along the way, but success combined with achievement is clearly within our grasp. It does not need to be difficult. We can all start by doing less, and then do less and less. We can work our way to the point of Doing Nothing and then we can take a vacation—without our cell phones.

These seven unnatural leaders are a tremendously diverse set of people: a salesman, a coach, an engineer, a musician, a Navy captain, a crusader, and a celebrity. They are interesting, inspiring people who have been incredibly effective. They exemplify and embody so many of the ideas in this book. They are **facilitators and orchestrators rather than being micromanagers**. They **focus on the task and on their people**, and they **care for them sincerely**. They often pull themselves out of the equation, which allows them to practice **the Leadership Law and focus on the reactions they are hoping for first**, rather than on their own actions. To do this well, they **get to know their people**, and they **act as their true friends**. They **give their team members voice**, they **help them to feel psychologically safe**, and they **trust them fully**.

They have simple schemes that allow them to *Do Nothing!* and thrive. All of us can also be better leaders and we can make our lives simpler and more meaningful at the same time. All we have to do is work toward *Doing Nothing!* to see how easy—and effective—it can be.

Acknowledgments

The journey to a book encompasses many events, large and small. Here are a few of the interactions that pushed me to write this book:

- More than a few years ago, after a session on leadership effectiveness, one of the executives in the class came up to me with a smile on his face. He said, "Why do people think that leadership is so hard?" He couldn't understand it, nor can I. It's not that we don't encounter difficult issues as leaders—it's just that, on a daily basis, many, many people make it harder than it has to be. We both agreed that leadership is easy and that it would be great if more people discovered this simple truth.

- "How many of you *Do Nothing*?" The odds of an affirmative answer to this question in my executive classes are about one in fifty (or less). But that one always accompanies a raised hand with a huge smile. *Do Nothing!* leaders look like the cat that just ate the canary—they have a self-satisfied look and the knowledge that they live in a dream world that makes everyone jealous.

- So many executives who love what they do have told me their stories. I wish I could thank each of them personally. Their challenges, their failures, and their inspiration have all been grist for my mill. They have been a constant source of insight, ideas, and affirmation. They have also provided tests for *Do Nothing!* ideas: their feedback indicates that doing less and less consistently works.

- I fell into the best job in the world. I'm surrounded by smart, motivated people who want to make the world a better place and who make my work life constantly challenging and interesting. My colleagues and my graduate students have pushed me, molded me, and influenced every aspect of how I think. I always hope that I have gotten better over time, and if that's true, they are the reason why. (I started to list their names here and then it seemed like I was hearing the music they play at the Academy Award shows when award recipients stay on too long. The list of people whom I should thank would be a *very* long list. Thus, rather than listing everyone here, I plan to seek everyone out to give each of them the personal thank-you that they deserve. I hope they don't mind not seeing their name here.)

Getting a book actually written sometimes seems like a Herculean task. Thus, there are several people who have been more recent influences. They have been *extremely* helpful in pushing me to actually reach closure and completion:

- Jim Levine, lover of books because he loves ideas and agent extraordinaire, suggested that this book be consistently contrarian, even though that's not my nature as a person. Couching each chapter title as being contrary to our natural inclinations, however, hit the nail on the head. Jim's sage direction was a godsend.

- Somebody out there likes what I write, and his name is Adrian Zackheim. I don't know why, and it's not because we have a strong personal connection, because we have not yet met. But who would ever predict that the first person to express confidence in my work, twenty years ago by publishing my first book, *Bargaining Games*, would also step up and publish this book, too. It's the kind of confidence booster that makes it easy to push ahead and actually finish the sometimes arduous job of writing.

- Is there a better publishing group than the folks at Portfolio / Penguin? Not as far as I can tell. Adrian, Will Weisser, Jillian Gray, Maureen Cole, Julia Batavia, and Michael Burke are not only on top of everything (e.g., they are wonderful facilitators and orchestrators), but they do it with verve and enthusiasm. I have not had this great an experience with a publisher in a long time. And is there a better agency than Levine Greenberg? Jim and his entire staff, especially Kerry Sparks, have been absolutely immediate in their assistance, advice, and support. They are amazing.

A final set of people are the constants in my life, the people who have always been there *whenever* I needed them. They are the reason for my very existence:

- Mom and Dad set the table of our lives and acted as the role models we always aspire to be. They did the right thing, over and over, even when it wasn't easy. They were incredible; we were blessed.

- Kev, Tom, and Peg, my awesome siblings, are a constant source of inspiration, friendship, and love. They have created a comfort zone for me for my entire life.
- Although having five children seems like it might be a formidable leadership challenge, my kids have been remarkably easy on me, and they always make me smile. Jack, Erik, Kate, Annie, and William are each, on their own, amazing gifts, to me and to the rest of the world.
- The best luck of my life has been the love of my life. Beth is as important to me as the oxygen I breathe.

The good part about thanks is that they are not exhaustible, and neither is my gratitude for all of these wonderful people.

I hope you like the book, and I hope it makes your life both more effective and easier. If it does, thank the people who made my life more effective and easier—without them I could not have accomplished this much. Also, thank the people who made your life more effective and easier—and tell me about them. I'd love to hear their stories!

Bibliography

Abadian, Susan. 1996. "Women's Autonomy and Its Impact on Fertility." *World Development* 24: 1793–1809.

Aumann, Robert J. 1995. "Backwards Induction and the Common Knowledge of Rationality." *Games and Economic Behavior* 8: 6–19.

Balkundi, Prasad, and David Harrison. 2006. "Ties, Leaders, and Time in Teams: Strong Inference About Network Structure's Effects on Team Viability and Performance." *Academy of Management Journal* 49: 49–68.

Baltes, Paul B., and K. Warner Schaie. 1976. "On the Plasticity of Intelligence in Adulthood and Old Age." *American Psychologist* 31: 720–25.

Bandura, Albert. 1997. *Self-Efficacy: The Exercise of Control.* New York: W. H. Freeman.

Baumeister, Roy F., Ellen Bratslavsky, Catrin Finkenauer, and Kathleen D. Vohs. 2001. "Bad Is Stronger Than Good." *Review of General Psychology* 5: 323–70.

Binet, Alfred. 1909, 1973. *Les Idées Modernes sur les Enfants (Modern Ideas About Children).* Paris: Flammarion.

Carter, Nancy L., and J. Mark Weber. 2010. "Not Pollyannas: Higher Generalized Trust Predicts Lie Detection Ability." *Social Psychological and Personality Science* 1 (3): 274–79.

206   Cialdini, Robert B. 2008. *Influence: Science and Practice*, 5th
      edition. Englewood Cliffs, N.J.: Prentice Hall.

Dickens, William T., and James R. Flynn. 2001. "Heritability
    Estimates vs. Large Environmental Effects: The IQ Paradox
    Resolved." *Psychological Review* 108: 346–69.

Diener, Ed, Weiting Ng, James Harter, and Raksha Arora. 2010.
    "Wealth and Happiness Across the World: Material Prosperity
    Predicts Life Evaluation, Whereas Psychosocial Prosperity
    Predicts Positive Feeling." *Journal of Personality and Social
    Psychology* 99: 52–61.

Dutta, Bhaskar, Matthew O. Jackson, and Michel Le Breton.
    2002. "Voting by Successive Elimination and Strategic
    Candidacy." *Journal of Economic Theory* 103: 190–218.

Dweck, Carol S. 2006. *Mindset.* New York: Random House.

Eden, Dov, and Abraham B. Shani. 1982. "Pygmalion Goes to
    Boot Camp: Expectancy, Leadership, and Trainee
    Performance." *Journal of Applied Psychology* 67: 194–99.

Edmondson, Amy C. 1999. "Psychological Safety and Learning
    Behavior in Work Teams." *Administrative Science Quarterly*
    44(4): 350–83.

Edmondson, Amy C. 2003. "Speaking Up in the Operating
    Room: How Team Leaders Promote Learning in
    Interdisciplinary Action Teams." *Journal of Management Studies*
    40: 1419–52.

Fincham, Frank, and Thomas Bradbury. 1989. "Perceived
    Responsibility for Marital Events: Egocentric or Partner-
    Centric Bias?" *Journal of Marriage and Family* 51: 27–35.

Fisher, Roger, and William L. Ury. 1981. *Getting to Yes.* New York:
    Penguin.

Flynn, James R. 1987. "Massive IQ Gains in 14 Nations: What IQ
    Tests Really Measure." *Psychological Bulletin* 101: 171–91.

Flynn, James R. 1999. "Searching for Justice: The Discovery of
    IQ Gains over Time." *American Psychologist* 54: 5–20.

Galinsky, Adam D., Joe C. Magee, Deborah H. Gruenfeld, Jennifer A. Whitson, and Katie A. Liljenquist. 2008. "Social Power Reduces the Strength of the Situation: Implications for Creativity, Conformity, and Dissonance." *Journal of Personality and Social Psychology* 95: 1450–66.

Galinsky, Adam D., Joe C. Magee, M. Ena Inesi, and Deborah H. Gruenfeld. 2006. "Power and Perspectives Not Taken." *Psychological Science* 17: 1068–74.

Gilbert, Daniel T., and Edward E. Jones. 1986. "Perceiver-Induced Constraint: Interpretations of Self-Generated Reality." *Journal of Personality and Social Psychology* 50: 269–80.

Gilovich, Thomas, Kenneth Savitsky, and Victoria Husted Medvec. 1998. "The Illusion of Transparency: Biased Assessments of Others' Ability to Read Our Emotional States." *Journal of Personality and Social Psychology* 75: 332–46.

Gilovich, Thomas, Victoria Husted Medvec, and Kenneth Savitsky. 2000. "The Spotlight Effect in Social Judgment: An Egocentric Bias in Estimates of the Salience of One's Own Actions and Appearance." *Journal of Personality and Social Psychology* 78: 211–22.

Ginzel, Linda. 1994. "The Impact of Biased Inquiry Strategies on Performance Judgments." *Organizational Behavior and Human Decision Processes* 33: 411–29.

Griffin, Dale W., and Lee Ross. 1991. "Subjective Construal, Social Inference, and Human Misunderstanding." In *Advances in Experimental Social Psychology*, edited by Mark P. Zanna, 24: 319–59. San Diego: Academic Press.

Gruenfeld, Deborah, Ena Inesi, Joe Magee, and Adam Galinsky. 2008. "Power and the Objectification of Social Targets." *Journal of Personality and Social Psychology* 95: 111–27.

Hackman, J. Richard. 2005. "A Theory of Team Coaching." *Academy of Management Review* 30: 269–87.

Harrison, Roger. 1976. "Role Negotiation: A Tough-Minded Approach to Team Development." In *Social Technology of Organization Development.* La Jolla, Calif.: University Associates.

Heslin, Peter A., and Don VandeWalle. 2008. "Managers' Implicit Assumptions About Personnel." *Current Directions in Psychological Science* 17: 219–23.

Heslin, Peter A., Don VandeWalle, and Gary P. Latham. 2006. "Keen to Help? Managers' IPTs and Their Subsequent Employee Coaching." *Personnel Psychology* 59: 871–902.

Heslin, Peter A., Gary P. Latham, and Don VandeWalle. 2005. "The Effect of Implicit Person Theory on Performance Appraisals." *Journal of Applied Psychology* 90: 842–56.

Hirschman, Albert O. 1970. *Exit, Voice, and Loyalty: Responses to Decline in Firms, Organizations, and States.* Cambridge, Mass.: Harvard University Press.

Hitchens, Christopher. "Believe Me, It's Torture." *Vanity Fair,* August 2008.

Horn, John L., and Gary Donaldson. 1976. "On the Myth of Intellectual Decline in Adulthood." *American Psychologist* 31: 701–19, 878.

Jussim, Lee. 1989. "Teacher Expectations: Self-fulfilling Prophecies, Perceptual Biases, and Accuracy." *Journal of Personality and Social Psychology* 57: 469–80.

Kahneman, Daniel, and Angus Deaton. 2011. "High Income Improves Evaluation of Life but Not Emotional Well-being. *Proceedings of the National Academy of Sciences* 107: 16489–93.

Kahneman, Daniel, and Jack L. Knetsch. 1991. "The Endowment Effect, Loss Aversion, and Status Quo Bias." *Journal of Economic Perspectives* 5: 193–206.

Kahneman, Daniel, Jack Knetsch, and Richard Thaler. 1991. "Anomalies: The Endowment Effect, Loss Aversion, and Status Quo Bias." *Journal of Economic Perspectives* 5: 193–206.

Knetsch, Jack L. 1989. "The Endowment Effect and Evidence of Nonreversible Indifference Curves." *American Economic Review* 79: 1277–84.

Kray, Laura, and Michael Haselhuhn. 2007. "Implicit Negotiation Beliefs and Performance: Longitudinal and Experimental Evidence." *Journal of Personality and Social Psychology* 93: 49–64.

Lawler, Edward E. III, Gerald E. Ledford, and Susan A. Mohrman. 1992. "Employee Involvement in America: Summary and Conclusions." *Quality and Productivity Management* 9: 71–75.

Lawler, Edward E. III, Susan A. Mohrman, and Gerald E. Ledford. 1998. *Strategies for High Performance Organizations: Employee Involvement, TQM, and Reengineering Programs in Fortune 1000 Corporations.* San Francisco: Jossey-Bass.

Levitt, Steven, John List, and Sally Sadoff. 2011. "Checkmate: Exploring Backward Induction Among Chess Players." *American Economic Review* 101: 975–90.

Lewis, Michael. 2010. *The Big Short: Inside the Doomsday Machine.* New York: W. W. Norton.

Libby, Robert, Ken Trotman, and Ian Zimmer. 1987. "Member Variation, Recognition of Expertise, and Group Performance." *Journal of Applied Psychology* 72: 81–87.

Locke, Edwin A., and Gary P. Latham. 1990. *Theory of Goal Setting and Task Performance.* Englewood Cliffs, N.J.: Prentice-Hall.

Locke, Edwin A., and Gary P. Latham. 2002. "Building a Practically Useful Theory of Goal Setting and Task Motivation." *American Psychologist* 57: 705–17.

Long, Christopher, and Susan Rose-Ackerman. 1982. "Winning the Contest by Agenda Manipulation." *Journal of Policy Analysis and Management* 2: 123–25.

Lowin, Aaron. 1968. "Participative Decision Making: A Model,
Literature Critique, and Prescriptions for Research."
Organizational Behavior and Human Performance 3: 68–106.

Malhotra, Deepak. 2004. "Trust and Reciprocity Decisions: The
Differing Perspectives of Trustors and Trusted Parties."
Organizational Behavior and Human Decision Processes
94: 61–73.

Mathieu, John E., and Dennis M. Zajac. 1990. "A Review and
Meta-analysis of the Antecedents Correlates and
Consequences of Organizational Commitment." *Psychological
Bulletin* 108: 171–99.

McNatt, D. Brian. 2000. "Ancient Pygmalion Joins
Contemporary Management: A Meta-analysis of the Result."
Journal of Applied Psychology 85: 314–22.

Messick, David, Suzanne Bloom, Janet Boldizar, and Charles
Samuelson. 1985. "Why We Are Fairer Than Others." *Journal
of Experimental Social Psychology* 21: 480–500.

Meyer, John P., and Natalie J. Allen. 1997. *Commitment in the
Workplace: Theory, Research, and Application.* Thousand Oaks,
Calif.: Sage.

Mintzberg, Henry. 1973. *The Nature of Managerial Work.* New
York: Harper & Row.

Mohrman, Susan A. 2008. "Leading Change: Do It with
Conversation." *Leadership Excellence* 25: 5.

Murnighan, J. K., and D. J. Conlon. 1991. "The Dynamics of
Intense Work Groups: A Study of British String Quartets."
Administrative Science Quarterly 36: 165–86.

Myerson, Debra, Karl E. Weick, and Roderick M. Kramer.
1990. "Swift Trust and Temporary Groups." In *Trust in
Organizations: Frontiers of Theory and Research,* edited by
Roderick M. Kramer and Tom R. Tyler. Thousand Oaks,
Calif.: Sage.

Neumann, John von, and Oskar Morgenstern. 1944. *The Theory of Games and Economic Behavior*. Princeton, N.J.: Princeton University Press.

Nietzsche, Friedrich. 1886, 1989. *Beyond Good and Evil: Prelude to a Philosophy of the Future*, translated by Walter Kaufmann. London: Vintage Books.

Nordgren, Loran F., Joop van der Pligt, and Frenk van Harreveld. 2007. "Evaluating Eve: Visceral States Influence the Evaluation of Impulsive Behavior." *Journal of Personality and Social Psychology* 93: 75–84.

Nordgren, Loran F., Kasia Banas, and Geoff MacDonald. 2011. "Empathy Gaps for Social Pain: Why People Underestimate the Pain of Social Suffering." *Journal of Personality and Social Psychology* 100: 120–28.

Ordóñez, Lisa D., Maurice E. Schweitzer, Adam D. Galinsky, and Max H. Bazerman. 2009. "On Good Scholarship, Goal Setting, and Scholars Gone Wild." *Academy of Management Perspectives* 23: 82–87.

Pillutla, Madan, Deepak Malhotra, and J. Keith Murnighan. 2003. "Attributions of Trust and the Calculus of Reciprocity." *Journal of Experimental Social Psychology* 39: 448–55.

Plott, Charles R., and Michael E. Levine. 1978. "A Model of Agenda Influence on Committee Decisions." *American Economic Review* 68: 146–60.

Quinn, Robert E. 1991. *Beyond Rational Management: Mastering the Paradoxes and Competing Demands of High Performance*. San Francisco: Jossey-Bass.

Ren, Yuqing, and Linda Argote. 2011. "Transactive Memory Systems 1985–2010: An Integrative Framework of Key Dimensions, Antecedents, and Consequences." In *The Academy of Management Annals*, edited by James P. Walsh and Arthur P. Brief, 5: 189–229. Philadelphia: Routledge.

Rosenthal, Robert A., and Lenore Jacobson. 1968. *Pygmalion in the Classroom: Teacher Expectations and Pupils' Intellectual Development.* New York: Holt, Rinehart, & Winston.

Ross, Michael, and Fiore Sicoly. 1979. "Egocentric Biases in Availability and Attribution." *Journal of Personality and Social Psychology* 37: 322–36.

Roth, Alvin E., and J. Keith Murnighan. 1982. "The Role of Information in Bargaining: An Experimental Study." *Econometrica* 50: 1123–42.

Ryan, Richard M., and Edward L. Deci. 2000. "Self-Determination Theory and the Facilitation of Intrinsic Motivation, Social Development, and Well-being." *American Psychologist* 55: 68–78.

Samuelson, William, and Richard J. Zeckhauser. 1988. "Status Quo Bias in Decision Making." *Journal of Risk and Uncertainty* 1: 7–59.

Shapira, Zur. 1997. *Risk Taking: A Managerial Perspective.* New York: Russell Sage Foundation.

Sivanathan, N., M. M. Pillutla, and J. K. Murnighan. 2008. "Power Gained, Power Lost." *Organizational Behavior and Human Decision Processes* 105: 135–46.

Smith, Adam. 1776, 2003. *The Wealth of Nations.* New York: Bantam.

Smith, Kenwyn, and David Berg. 1987. *Paradoxes of Group Life.* San Francisco: Jossey-Bass.

Sparrow, Betsy, Jenny Liu, and Daniel M. Wegner. 2011. "Google Effects on Memory: Cognitive Consequences of Having Information at Our Fingertips." *Science* 333: 776–78.

Spencer, Steven J., Claude M. Steele, and Diane M. Quinn. 1999. "Stereotype Threat and Women's Math Performance." *Journal of Experimental Social Psychology* 35: 4–28.

Steele, Claude M., Steven J. Spencer, and Joshua Aronson. 2002. "Contending with Group Image: The Psychology of

Stereotype and Social Identity Threat." *Advances in Experimental Social Psychology* 34: 379–440.

Taylor, Shelley, and Jonathan Brown. 1988. "Illusion and Well-being: A Social Psychological Perspective on Mental Health." *Psychological Bulletin* 103: 193–210.

Ury, William L. 1991, 2007. *Getting Past No.* New York: Bantam.

van Kleef, Gerben A., Christopher Oveis, Ilmo van der Lowe, Aleksandr Luo Kogan, Jennifer Goetz, and Dacher Keltner. 2008. "Power, Distress, and Compassion: Turning a Blind Eye to the Suffering of Others." *Psychological Science* 19: 1315–22.

Wang, Cynthia S., Adam D. Galinsky, and J. Keith Murnighan. 2009. "Bad Drives Psychological Evaluations but Good Propels Behavior: Responses to Honesty and Deception." *Psychological Science* 20: 634–44.

Wang, Long. 2009. "Money and Fame: Vividness Effects in the National Basketball Association." *Journal of Behavioral Decision Making* 20: 20–44.

Weber, J. Mark, Deepak Malhotra, and J. Keith Murnighan. 2005. "Normal Acts of Irrational Trust: Motivated Attributions and the Trust Development Process." In *Research in Organizational Behavior*, vol. 26, edited by Barry M. Staw and Roderick M. Kramer, 75–102. New York: Elsevier.

Wegner, Daniel M. 1986. "Transactive Memory: A Contemporary Analysis of the Group Mind." In *Theories of Group Behavior*, edited by Brian Mullen and George R. Goethals, 185–208. New York: Springer-Verlag.

Wegner, Daniel M., Toni Giuliano, and Paula Hertel. 1985. "Cognitive Interdependence in Close Relationships." In *Compatible and Incompatible Relationships*, edited by William J. Ickes, 253–76. New York: Springer-Verlag.

Wickersham Commission, The. 1931. "Report on Lawlessness in Law Enforcement."

Index

Abrashoff, Michael, 187–89
Do Nothing! practices of, 50, 135,
    188–89, 198
Active listening
  benefits of, 48
  technique for, 48, 53–54
Acton, Lord, 26
Agenda, 119–21
  as decision-making tool, 120–21
  effectiveness of, 119–20
  as structural control tool, 119–20
Amadeus String Quartet, Brainin
  as leader, 183–87
Appeasement, and Chamberlain's
  leadership, 35–38
Artest, Ron, 178
*Art of High-States Decision-Making:
  Tough Calls in a Speed-Driven
  World* (Murnighan and
  Mowen), 121

Backwards induction, 69–75
  Clinton, Bill, 72–73
  effectiveness of, 71–72, 74–75

versus next step
  approach, 67–69
university president
  example, 69–72
Balcony, getting on, 49–50
Bargaining Games
  (Murnighan), 203
Berra, Yogi, 164, 165
Big Short, The (Lewis), 159–60
Binet, Alfred, 144
Blame
  versus apologizing, 87–88
  fundamental attribution
    error, 39
BlinkNow Foundation, Doyne as
  leader, 189–93
Brainin, Norbert, 183–87
  Do Nothing! practices of,
    185–87, 198
Brown, Michael, Hurricane Katrina
  mismanagement, 45–47
Bryant, Kobe, 178
Buffett, Warren, 167
Bush, George W., 22

Cardiac surgery team, as
democratic team, 111–15
Caring by leader, 132–37
friendship with team
members, 135–36
socializing with team, 134
tough love, 135
Carter, Nancy, 89
CDW (Computer Discount
Warehouse), Krasny as
leader, 157, 172–75
Chamberlain, Neville,
appeasement plan
fiasco, 35–38
Change
resistance to, 5–6
See also Learning
Cheney, Dick, 22
Chicago Bulls
dirty work, 65–67
Jackson as leader, 175–79
roles/skills diversity,
coordinating, 59–60
Churchill, Winston, and
appeasement fiasco, 35–38
Cialdini, Bob, 108
Clinton, Bill, 72–73
Communication
active listening, 48
transparency effect, 32–34
Comparative advantage, 6–7
Control, taking
Leadership Dilemma, 116, 118
as leadership problem,
105–7, 116–18

as natural reaction, 116
solution to. See Democratic work
teams; Structural control
Corbally, John, 118–19
Creativity
and growth mind-set, 148
ideas, weeding out, 182
Criticism
giving, and structural
control, 122–23
questions instead of, 123, 182
ulterior motives accusation, 123

Decision-making, agenda
as tool, 120–21
Defective products, correcting,
motivation for, 128–30
Democratic work teams, 107–16
cardiac surgery teams example,
111–15
characteristics of, 108, 117
limitations of, 108
voice, having in, 109–11, 117
Dirty work, 65–67, 129
by leader, 13
necessity of, 65–67
rotation scheme for, 13
sports team example, 65–67
and subordinate goals, 129
Division of labor, roles/skills
diversity, recognizing/
coordinating, 57–62
Do Nothing! leadership
Abrashoff, Michael, 50, 135,
187–89, 198

avoiding, situations for, 12–14
basic concept of, 4–10
comparative advantage
　related to, 6–7
difficulty of, 10–12
Doyne, Maggie, 189–93, 199
as enhanced leadership, 4
Honda, Soichiro, 179–83, 197
Jackson, Phil, 59–60, 65–67,
　175–79, 197
Krasny, Michael, 157–59,
　172–75, 196–97
litmus test for, 18–19
Norbert, Brainin, 183–87, 198
traits of leader, 8–9, 133,
　135, 171–72
Winfrey, Oprah, 193–97, 199
See also Leadership solutions
Double interacts, 38–39
Doyne, Maggie, 189–93
　Do Nothing! practices of,
　191–93, 199
Dweck, Carol, 144–45, 150–51

Eastman Kodak Company, 4
EBay, buying, trust factor, 78–80, 82
Economic crisis, factors in,
　159–60, 168
Edmondson, Amy, 111–15
Edwardson, John, 174
Egalitarian teams. *See* Democratic
　work teams
Egocentrism, 27–29
　Chamberlain and appeasement
　fiasco, 35–38

as leadership problem, 27–29
　solution to, 42–43
Emerson, Ralph Waldo, 193
Empathy gap, 22–29
　and egocentrism, 28–29
　-power combination, dangers
　of, 25–26
　research studies related
　to, 23–25
　solution to, 43–45
Expectations
　of leader, positive impact of,
　16–17
　positive reactions,
　benefits of, 47
　Pygmalion Effect, 15–16
　of team members, clarity of, 58

Facilitators, leaders as, 8, 9,
　13–14, 136
Fatigue, and empathy gap, 23–25
Fear, and lack of trust, 81–86,
　99–100, 102–3
Fisher, Roger, 49
Fitch, Bill, 175
Fixed mind-set, 144–47
　characteristics of, 144–45
　and lying, 147
　reverse of. *See* Growth mind-set
　talent versus effort, 145–47
Flynn, James, 142–43
Fujisawa, Takeo, 181, 183, 197
Fundamental attribution error
　defined, 39
　as leadership problem, 39

Galinsky, Adam, 43–44
Game theory, backwards
    induction, 69–75
Gates, Bill, 141
General Electric, 63
George VI, king of England,
    36–37
Getting Past No (Ury), 49
Getting to Yes (Ury and
    Fisher), 49
Gilovich, Tom, 32–33
Goals, 62–75
    Clinton, Bill, achievement
        of, 72–73
    next step, backwards
        induction, 67–75
    personal goals, 67, 74
    and structural control, 123
    subordinate goals, importance
        of, 64–67, 128–30
    team goals, characteristics
        of, 63–65
Goldsmith, Jack, 22
Golf, 138–39
Grant, Harvey, 66–67
Grant, Horace, 60, 65, 65–67
GrassRoots Leadership, 188
Griffin, Dale, 33
Growth mind-set, 141–56
    adopting, steps in, 148
    "born versus made" leader,
        141–44
    versus fixed mind-set, 144–50
    IQ, gains over lifetime, 142–44

perseverance, 149–50
    Post-Project Evaluation
        Meetings (PPEMs), 152–54
    and team, promoting, 150–56

Harpo Inc., Winfrey as
    leader, 193–97
Haselhuhn, Michael, 147
Hatvany, Nina, 149–50
Heslin, Peter, 148–49
Hitler, Adolf, Chamberlain and
    appeasement fiasco, 35–38
Holzman, Red, 175
Honda, Soichiro, 179–83
    Do Nothing! practices of,
        181–83, 197
Honda Motor Company, Honda
    as leader, 179–83
Hull, Raymond, 141–42
Hurricane Katrina,
    mismanagement of, 45–47

Incentive systems, as structural
    control tool, 120–21
Influence (Cialdini), 108
Intelligence tests (IQ), gains over
    lifetime, 142–44
Interrogation methods
    and empathy gap, 22–23
    waterboarding, 22–24, 27
Intuition, and trust, 81
It's Your Ship (Abrashoff), 50,
    135, 189
Iverson, Allen, 146

Jackson, Phil, 175–79
    Do Nothing! practices of, 59–60,
        65–67, 177–79, 197
Jones, Jerry, 100
Jordan, Michael, 59–60, 178
Joyce, James, 47

Kelleher, Herb, 50
Kerr, Steve, 60
Kopila Valley Children's Home,
    Doyne as leader, 189–93
Kopila Valley Primary School,
    Doyne as leader, 189–93
Kraemer, Harry, 123
Krasny, Michael, 172–75
    Do Nothing! practices of,
        157–59, 173–74, 196–97
Kray, Laura, 147
Krzyzewski, Mike, 42–43

Leaders
    as facilitators, 8, 9,
        13–14, 136
    great, characteristics of, 8–9,
        133, 135, 171–72
    as "lonely" saying, 127,
        128, 136
    as orchestrators, 8, 9,
        13–14, 136
    problems/solutions related to.
        See Leadership problems;
        Leadership solutions
    as wire walkers, 125
    See also Do Nothing! leadership

Leadership Law, 31–32, 45
Leadership problems, 21–54
    actions, misperception of
        impact of, 29–32, 38–40
    Brown, Michael, 45–47
    Bush administration, 22–23
    Chamberlain, Neville, 35–38
    change, resistance to, 5–6
    control issue, 105–7, 116–18
    doing too much, 2–3, 8, 102
    egocentrism, 27–29, 35
    empathy gap, 22–29
    fixed mind-set, 144–47
    fundamental attribution
        error, 39
    Leadership Dilemma, 116, 118
    micromanagers, 7, 102
    performance goals, 137–40
    Peter Principle, 6, 141–42
    power, 25–28
    profit maximization, 160–63
    Pygmalion Effect, 14–16
    self-fulfilling prophecy, 40–41
    solutions to. *See Do Nothing!*
        leadership; Leadership
        solutions
    technical skills, giving
        up, 11–12
    transparency effect, 32–34
    trust, lack of, 81–86
Leadership solutions, 42–54
    active listening, 47–48, 53–54
    caring about people, 132–37
    democratic work teams, 107–16

Leadership solutions (cont.)
    focus on others, 42–43, 52–53
    "get on the balcony," 49–50
    goals, awareness of, 29, 62–75
    growth mind-set, 141–56
    Leadership Law, 31–32, 45
    perspective taking, 43–45, 53
    psychological safety,
        creating, 114–15
    reactions of others,
        predicting, 47, 53
    right-hand man, role of,
        181–83, 197
    structural control, 118–23
    task-orientation, 126–32
    team skills/roles,
        coordinating, 57–62
    trust more, 80–103
    value maximization, 162–63
    values, 163–69
    "walking the floor," 50–51
    See also Do Nothing! leadership
Learning
    goals, importance of, 140–41
    growth mind-set, 141–56
    IQ, gains over lifetime,
        142–44
    lifelong learning, 141
    from mistakes, 47, 152–53
    and self-discovery, 121
    skills of team, expanding, 12,
        62, 140–41
    by trusting, 88–91
Lewis, Michael, 159–60
Listening. See Active listening

Lovett, Martin, 184
Lying, and fixed mind-set, 147

McCain, John, 22
Medvec, Vicki, 32–33
Meetings
    agenda as tool, 119–21
    Post-Project Evaluation
        Meetings (PPEMs), 152–54
Micromanagers, 7, 102
Mission statement, as structural
        control tool, 122
Mistakes
    apologizing, benefits of, 87–88
    learning from, 47, 152–53
    Post-Project Evaluation
        Meetings (PPEMs), 152–54
Mohammed, Khalid Sheikh, 22
Motivation, and subordinate
        goals, 64–66, 129
Mowen, John, 121

Negotiation
    competitive versus cooperative,
        31–32, 38, 49
    fixed versus growth mind-set
        in, 147–48
Newtonian leadership, 29–30
Nietzsche, Friedrich, 120
Nissel, Siegmund, 184
Nordgren, Loren, 23–25

Objectivity, mental distancing,
        methods for, 49–51
O'Neal, Shaquille, 178

Orchestrators, leaders as, 8, 9, 13–14, 136
Orienteering challenge, 105–7
Outcomes, control, lack of, 154–56

Participation, equal. *See* Democratic work teams
Performance
   versus effort.
      See Growth mind-set
   excellence, rewarding, 51
   outcomes, lack of control of, 154–56
Performance goals, 137–41
   criteria for, 137–38
   golf game example, 138–39
   versus learning goals, 140–41
   limitations of, 137–40, 144–45
Perseverance, 149–50
Perspective taking
   benefits of, 45, 53
   versus egocentrism, 27–29
   versus empathy gap, 22–29
   and power, 43–45
   steps in, 43–45
Peter, Dr. Laurence, 141–42
Peter Principle, 6, 141–42
Pippen, Scottie, 59–60, 178
Pluralistic ignorance, 115
Post-Project Evaluation Meetings (PPEMs), 152–54
Power, 25–28
   and corruption, 26
   -empathy gap combination, 25–26

   as leadership problem, 26–28
   and perspective taking, 43–45
   and transparency effect, 34
Predicting behavior
   by leader, 47, 53
   and structural control, 120–22
Pride, team members, 56
Prisoners, Stanford prison experiment, 25–26
Profit maximization
   and economic crisis, 159–60, 168
   problems of, 160–62
   versus value maximization, 162–63
Promotion
   giving up past, 16, 18
   new leader, learning about team, 92–99
   new skills, exercising, 6
   reasons for, 117
Psychological safety
   creating, 114–15
   and work teams, 114–15
Pygmalion Effect
   fictional basis of, 15
   research studies related to, 15–16
   solution to, 47

Questions
   asking, benefits of, 42–43
   encouraging, with psychological safety, 114–15
   to uncover flaws, 123, 182

Rational model, of trust
    development, 86–88
Reactions
    double interacts, 38–39
    leader actions, misperception
        of impact, 29–32
    Leadership Law, 31–32
    predicting, benefits of, 47, 53
Reciprocity, and trust, 84–85, 99
Rewards
    for educational experiences, 151
    for excellent performance, 51
    as structural control tool, 120–21
Risk, and trust, 81–82, 85, 99–103
Rodman, Dennis, 60, 178
Rogers, Carl, 47–48
Ross, Lee, 33
Rostal, Max, 184

Sacred Hoops: Spiritual Lessons
    of a Hardwood Warrior
    (Jackson), 176
Safety, psychological, 114–15
Savitsky, Ken, 32–33
Schidlof, Peter, 184
Schulz, Charles, 130
Self-discovery, and learning
    process, 121
Self-fulfilling prophecy
    defined, 40
    as leadership problem, 40–41
    solution to, 47
Smith, Adam, 160
Social activity, leadership as, 27
Southwest Airlines, 50

Stanford prison experiment,
    25–26
Status quo bias, 4
Steinbrenner, George, 100
Sternberg, Robert, 149
Structural control, 118–23
    agenda, use of, 119–20
    defined, 120
    effectiveness of, 120–23
    and goals, 123
    incentive systems as, 120–21
    mission statements as, 122
    and predicting behavior,
        120–22
Subordinate goals
    importance of, 64–67
    motivation, increasing with, 129
    types of, 64

Task orientation
    defect rate correction example,
        128–30
    dental workshop example,
        130–32
    extra homework example,
        127–28
    and leadership effectiveness,
        126–32
    versus performance goals,
        137–40
    speed of task, improving,
        130–32
    team, pushing to do more,
        126–32
    tough love, 135

Team/team members
  authority, giving by leader,
    55–56
  caring by leader, 132–37
  democratic work teams, 107–16
  dirty work, 13
  goals, 63–67
  growth mind-set, promoting,
    150–56
  leader expectations, clarity of, 58
  learning, encouraging, 13, 62,
    140–41
  new leader, learning about
    team, 92–99
  observing/"getting on the
    balcony," 49–50
  positive spirit, conditions
    for, 61–62
  pride, benefits of, 56
  professionals, positive
    outcomes from, 84
  psychological safety, 114–15
  rewards, 51, 120–21, 151
  skill diversity, recognizing/
    coordinating, 57–62
  socializing with team, 134
  task orientation,
    benefits of, 126–32
  traits needed, 59
  transactive memory, 58
  unassigned roles, caution
    about, 61
  values, sharing with, 165–68
Tough love, 135
Transactive memory, 58

Transparency effect, 32–34
  defined, 32–33
  as leadership problem, 32–34
  and power, 34
  research studies related to, 33
Trust, 80–103
  blind, avoiding, 82–83
  development, rational model,
    86–88
  diversifying, 101–2
  earning trust, pitfalls of, 94–97
  eBay experience, 78–80, 82
  and fear, 81–86, 99–100, 102–3
  and intuition, 81
  knowledge as basis of,
    82–83, 95–96
  and leadership effectiveness,
    80–81, 84–85, 91, 96–99,
    101–2
  and learning, 88–91
  new leader/new team, 96–99
  over trusting, 87–88
  partial trust, pitfalls of,
    100–101
  and reciprocity, 84–85, 99
  and risk, 81–82, 85, 99–103
  trustworthiness, most people, 91
  violations, impact of, 83–84
Tullman, Glen, 151
Twain, Mark, 143

University president
  backwards induction toward
    job of, 69–72
  leading, key to, 119

Ury, William, 49
USS *Benfold*, Abrashoff as captain,
    50–51, 187–89

Value maximization
    benefits of, 163, 167
    versus profit maximization,
        162–63
Values, 163–69
    awareness, and behavior,
        164–65, 168–69
    sharing with team, 165–68

Waterboarding
    and empathy gap,
        22–23, 25, 27
    as interrogation method,
        22–24

Wealth of Nations, The
    (Smith), 160
Weber, Mark, 89
Wegner, Daniel, 58
Weick, Karl, 38–39, 41
Welch, Jack, 123
Winfrey, Oprah, 193–97
    Do Nothing! practices of,
        194–96, 199
Workaholics, versus leaders, 3
World War II, Chamberlain and
    appeasement fiasco, 35–38

Yaokasin, Jimmy, 133
Young Presidents' Organization
    (YPO), 166

Zimbardo, Philip, 25–26